THE PRENUP GIRL PRESENTS

The Prenup Girl's Guide to a Successful Marriage

Carlie Spencer
Olivia Reiff

the prenup girl
WITH STRIVE LAW FIRM

COPYRIGHT © 2024 STRIVE LAW FIRM
All rights reserved.

THE PRENUP GIRL'S GUIDE
TO A SUCCESSFUL MARRIAGE

First Edition

ISBN 979-8-218-53857-6 (paperback)
ISBN 979-8-218-53858-3 (ebook)

Dedicated to:

Jeff Bezos and MacKenzie Scott
Married 1993-2019

Let these two serve as a cautionary tale of why a land with no prenups can be scary ... for Bezos ... kudos to MacKenzie.

Table of Contents

Introduction	1
Chapter 1	9
Chapter 2	23
Chapter 3	44
Chapter 4	56
Chapter 5	60
Chapter 6	64
Chapter 7	79
Conclusion	101
Appendix A	105
Appendix B	108
Appendix C	115

Introduction

Hey there, Lovebirds! So, you are thinking about tying the knot, huh? Congrats! Marriage is a big, exciting step. While you are dreaming about your happily ever after, do not forget you need to chat about something that might seem a little less romantic and sexy, but is actually incredibly important—prenuptial agreements, or prenups, as we like to call them. Thankfully, you have come to the right place!

Hi! I'm Carlie, the Prenup Girl. My goal in this book is to guide you (and hopefully your soon-to-be-betrothed) through the importance of prenups. We will discuss how to collaborate with your partner for your mutual financial success in marriage, provide you with resources to communicate with your partner, and explain what a lawyer needs to know in order to help you execute a top notch prenup.

What is a Prenup, anyway? Great question! Black's Law Dictionary (12th ed. 2024) defines a prenuptial agreement as follows:

> *Prenuptial Agreement: (1882) An agreement made before marriage usually to resolve issues of support and property division if the marriage ends in divorce or by the death of a spouse. — Also termed antenuptial agreement; antenuptial contract; premarital agreement; premarital contract; marriage settlement. — Sometimes shortened to prenup.*

Boring! Look, we all know lawyers are stereotypically very formal, often stuffy, or even pretentious. Yes, I said it and I mean it. But thankfully, there is a new wave of fresh attorneys that want to be different. These are attorneys who want to meet clients on their level and talk to them like humans, rather than trying to speak like a haughty theologian. I'm one of those types of new attorneys. So, throughout this book, I will do my best to explain legal concepts in detail, but also break things down the best way that I can so that it actually makes sense, does not bore you to tears, and does not want to make you want to throw this book across the room.

So where were we? Oh yeah! What is a prenup? Picture this: you have just bought your dream house, started a business, or maybe you are bringing a family heirloom into the marriage (like Grandma's vintage cookie jar). A prenup is like your personal love contract that helps sort out the nitty-gritty stuff if life takes a turn that you did not expect. Think of it as a financial game plan. It is not about being negative. It is about being smart!

Let's talk about money. That is right, you will have to think and talk about money quite a bit in this process. And this is true whether you have a lot of jingle in your pocket, or none at all. (Don't worry, it also applies if your bank accounts are somewhere in the middle.). One of the best things about a prenup preparation is that it gets you talking about money in detail with your partner. I know, not the most thrilling topic, but it is imperative you do so in order to have a successful financial future together. Having a prenup means you will hold those deep, meaningful conversations about who is paying for what and what happens if something goes awry. I cannot tell you the number of times I have heard a client say, "Oh, yeah! We have already had those tough convos. We are going to have joint finances and split everything! We just need to get it in writing and sign the prenup!" In mere minutes, I uncover, that besides agreeing to "joint finances" and "splitting everything," these couples have rarely discussed any additional details and have not, in fact, had any of the tough conversations. Instead, they have had only cursory and surface level conversations. Splitting finances can mean an even or equal 50/50 split of expenses, it can be based on the percentage income and earnings each person brings in, etc. And what does having "joint finances" even mean?

I could go on for hours with all the various ways couples can have "joint finances," but I digress for now and will address that later in this handy dandy book. Ultimately, discussing and executing a prenup is like financial couples therapy–only without the couch.

An Advantage of Getting a Prenup: Keeping What's Yours, Well, As Yours

Imagine you have got a killer vintage car, or maybe you are the proud owner of a sprawling collection of comic books or action figures. A prenup helps keep those personal treasures safe, making sure they stay with you if things do not go as planned. It is like having a protective bubble around your prized possessions.

Debts? No Thanks!

We all know someone who has a mountain of student loans or a credit card bill that is out of control–maybe it is you or your fiancé. A prenup can keep your partner from being dragged into that financial mess. So, if you are marrying someone with a less-than-stellar credit history, a prenup helps ensure you do not end up paying for their shopping sprees or student loans. It is like having a financial safety net.

Save The Drama for Your Llama

Nobody wants to think about divorce when they are getting married, but if it ever happens, a prenup is a guidebook that is already set up. It tells you and your partner what happens to your stuff and how things will be handled. This way, if things do not work out, you have already got a plan and can avoid messy arguments and court drama. It is like having a get-out-of-jail-free card for financial disputes. (I like to think that Mr. Monopoly also endorses prenups.)

Let the Prenup be a Referee in Your Marriage (just without the whistle)

A prenup is not about being suspicious or untrusting. It is about making sure both partners feel secure and respected. It is a way to show that you are planning for your future together in a fair and honest way. Think of it as setting the ground rules for a really long and happy game of Life. And you both get to agree on the rules of the game before you even start playing.

***

Let's clear the air. Prenups are not just for the rich, or for people who expect their marriage to fail. They are for everyone who wants to make sure they are on the same page about finances. They are practical, helpful, and totally normal. It is like having an insurance policy for your relationship—nobody wants to use it, but you are glad you have it if you need it.

There you have it! Prenups might not be the most romantic part of getting married, but they are definitely one of the smartest. They help you and your partner navigate the tricky parts of life with clarity and confidence. Next time someone brings up prenups, just remember it is not about doom and gloom, but about planning for a future that is as bright as your love story.

***

Busting Myths: Let's Get Real About Prenups

Alright, let's get something straight—prenups have a bad rep, and it is time we clear that up. You have probably heard all sorts of things about them, like they are only for rich folks or that they suck the romance right out of a relationship. Well, buckle up, because we are about to bust those myths wide open!

Myth #1: Prenups Are Only for the Rich and Famous

Okay, I get it. When you think of prenups, you might picture some Hollywood celebrity protecting their millions. But guess what? Prenups are for everyone! You do not need to be rolling in dough to benefit from one. Think of it this way: even if you are bringing a modest nest egg into your marriage, a prenup can help make sure it stays safe and sound. It is like having a personalized financial security blanket.

And prenups can address more than just the cash. Got a quirky collection of vinyl records? A beloved pet? A small business you have been nurturing? A prenup ensures that your treasures stay yours, no matter what. It is about protecting what is important to you, whether it is a vintage car or your grandmother's heirloom jewelry.

Myth #2: Prenups Are Unromantic

Ah, the big one. "Prenups are so unromantic!" Let's be real for a second—talking about money and future what-ifs might not sound like the stuff of fairy tales, but neither is fighting over finances down the line. Having a prenup is like having a heart-to-heart about your future. It is showing that you care enough to plan ahead and make sure neither of you gets hurt if things do not go as planned. Think of it like this: planning a wedding is not just about the dress and the cake ... it is about setting yourselves up for a happy, healthy marriage. A prenup is part of that plan. Plus, talking about a prenup can actually bring you closer. You will learn more about each other's financial habits, dreams, and even fears. Now, how is that for bonding?

Myth #3: Prenups Mean You Don't Trust Each Other

Let's squash this myth right now. A prenup does not mean that you do not trust your partner; it means you are both smart enough to prepare for all possible futures. You do not have car insurance because you are expecting to get into an accident on the road. But you have it, and are happy to have it, just in case. A prenup is like relationship insurance.

By discussing and signing a prenup, you are saying, "I love you so much that I want to make sure we are both protected, no matter what happens." It is a gesture of love, trust, and mutual respect that shows that you are both mature enough to handle serious conversations about the future.

Myth #4: Prenups Are All About Divorce

Sure, prenups are often brought up in the context of divorce, but they are not only for divorce. A prenup can cover all sorts of things, not just what happens if you split up. It can outline how you will handle finances during your marriage, what happens if one of you gets into debt, and even how you will manage things if one of you decides to take a break from work to raise kids. It is all about creating a solid financial plan that works for both of you.

Prenups are really about setting clear, fair expectations from the get-go. It is like having a map for your financial journey together. This way, you know exactly where you are going and how you are going to get there together.

Myth #5: Prenups Are Complicated and Expensive

Let's keep it real. Getting a prenup does not have to break the bank or require a law degree. Sure, you will need a lawyer to help you draft it but think of it as an investment in your future. The peace of mind you will get knowing that you are both on the same page financially is worth every penny. Plus, there are plenty of resources out there to help you understand the process and make it as smooth as possible.

***

So, there you have it! Prenups are not just for the rich, the paranoid, or the unromantic. They are for anyone who wants to enter marriage with eyes wide open and a plan in place. By busting these myths, we hope you see prenups for what they really are: a smart, loving way to protect yourselves and each other.

Next time someone tells you that prenups are a buzzkill, just smile and tell them you are planning for a love that is built to last. Read on for more prenup wisdom coming your way—because you have got this, and we are here to help every step of the way!

Chapter 1

Understanding Prenuptial Agreements

Welcome to the wonderful world of prenups! I know, I know—when you think about wedding planning, you are probably picturing cake tastings and dance lessons, not legal documents. But trust me, understanding prenups is one of the best things that you can do for your future together. So, grab a cup of coffee (or a glass of wine if we are being honest), and let's dive into the what, why, and how of prenups!

What's a Prenup, Anyway?

Let's start with the basics. A prenuptial agreement is a fancy legal term for a contract that two people sign before they get married. It is a plan for your financial future together. This document spells out how you will handle your money, property, debts, businesses, and more if things do not go exactly as planned. And I do not just mean the D-word of divorce ... I also mean in the event of death. Of course, you do not want to think about death or divorce, but anything is possible. You should be prepared for all outcomes, including a lifelong, loving marriage. So, take a few minutes off from engagement bliss and wedding planning to think about the very serious and real scenarios that we all hope you will never have to experience.

Imagine you are building a house together. You would not start without a solid blueprint, right? A prenup is the blueprint for your marriage's financial foundation. It helps you to both understand what to expect and how to navigate the occasionally hazardous waters of money matters.

***

The Purpose of a Prenup: Why Bother?

You might be thinking, "Why do we even need this?" Great question! Here is the scoop:

Clarity and Transparency:

A prenup forces you to have those important money conversations before you say, "I do." You will discuss assets, debts, and financial goals, making sure there are no surprises down the road. It is like a financial heart-to-heart. I cannot tell you the amount of "joint finances fiancés" I meet who do not have a clue what that means. Throughout the prenup planning process you will get clarity on all the financial decisions you and your partner need to walk into your marriage.

Protection:

Let's say you have got a killer art collection or a family business you are super proud of. A prenup ensures that these things stay yours if things go south. It is like a security system for your prized possessions. Even though you will likely merge some of your individual assets during the marriage, you may have some assets you want to protect. Talk it out together.

Debt Shielding:

Got student loans? Credit card debt? A prenup can protect you from taking on your partner's debt if the marriage does not work out. Think of it as a financial raincoat—you stay dry even if there is a storm.

Peace of Mind:

Imagine this: you are cuddled up on the couch with your partner and buttery popcorn, binge-watching Sex and the City for the hundredth time, and you just feel comfy and content. Not only because of the show (although, hey, who does not love a good Netflix marathon?), but because you know you have got your financial ducks in a row. That is what a prenup gives you—peace of mind.

Life is full of unexpected twists and turns. But, when you have taken the time to plan your financial future together, you have created a safety net that catches you both if things ever get tough. This is not about expecting the worst—it is about being smart, proactive, and making sure that your love story is supported by a strong, stable foundation. When you know that you have got a plan in place, it is like a weight has been lifted off your shoulders. No more lying awake at night worrying about "what if" scenarios. Instead, you can focus on what really matters: the love, joy, and connection that brought you together in the first place. Your prenup is there to catch you if you ever need it. Just like a good insurance policy, you hope you will never have to use it, but it is comforting to know that it is there.

With a prenup, you have already mapped out how to handle your finances, property, and even debts if life throws you a curveball. This safety net is not just for "worst-case scenarios" like divorce or death. It can also cover things like illness, job loss, if one parent will stay home with the children, or other financial challenges that might come up during your marriage. Knowing that you have thought ahead and planned for these possibilities means you can relax and enjoy your life together.

***

What Does a Prenup Cover?

Prenups are not one-size-fits-all. If you talk to a lawyer that tells you that ... May I respectfully suggest you run away? Prenups can be as simple or as detailed as you need them to be. Sure, there are certain standard clauses, but every single couple and individual that gets a prenup will have completely different assets, debts, and goals.

Here is a list of some common things prenups can cover and the questions you should be able to answer before tying the knot:

Assets and Property
- Who owns assets that come into the marriage?
- Do you share all financial accounts?
- If you have a mixture of joint and separate assets, how will you handle maintenance of the separate assets?
- What happens to these things if you split?
- Will inheritances be considered separate or marital property?
- How will you handle gifts received during the marriage?
- What happens to the marital home if you separate?
- How will other significant assets (e.g., cars, investments) be divided?
- How will you handle big financial decisions, like buying a home or investing?

Debts
- Who is responsible for pre-existing debt?
- How will debts be paid?
- Will one partner pay off the other's debt?
- Will only the indebted partner make payments on their debt?
- Will each partner contribute a percentage to the debt payments?
- How will new debt incurred during the marriage be managed?

- What happens if one partner accumulates significant debt during the marriage?

Income and Expenses
- How will you handle joint expenses?
- Will you have joint bank accounts, or keep things separate?
- Do you put both of your full incomes into the same joint account?
- Do you contribute a percentage of your individual incomes into a joint account and also have separate accounts?
- How do you budget and save for big purchases?
- How will household expenses be divided?
- How will future earnings, bonuses, and raises be treated?

Spousal Support
- Will one of you pay spousal support if you divorce?
- If so, how much and for how long?

Business Interests
- If one partner owns a business, how will it be managed?
- If one partner owns a business, will the other have any claim to it?
- How will the business be valued and divided if you split?

Life Events
- What happens if one of you wants to go back to school or change careers?

- How will you manage finances during significant life events, such as having children, buying a home, or moving to a new city?
- Will one partner's career sacrifices (e.g., for raising children) be compensated?
- How will retirement accounts be divided?
- Will both partners contribute equally to retirement savings, or will one contribute more?
- How will assets be distributed if one partner passes away?
- Do you have or plan to create a will that aligns with your prenup?

If you are unable to answer a majority of those questions, you need to sit down with your partner. Don't be scared! That was a lot of questions. You probably couldn't answer them all, but that is why you have this book now!!

***

Creating a prenup is about setting yourselves up for success. Here is how to make creating a prenup a smooth process:

Start Early: Don't wait until the last minute. Give yourselves plenty of time to discuss, draft, negotiate, and review the agreement.

Be Honest: Lay all your financial cards on the table. Honesty is the best policy, and it'll help you both make informed decisions.

Get Legal Help: A prenup is a legal document, so it is a good idea to have lawyers involved. They will make sure everything is fair and legally sound.

Communicate: Keep the lines of communication open. This is about building a strong foundation together, so make sure you are both comfortable with the terms.

And hey, let's keep it light! Think of a prenup like a relationship user manual. You would not use a fancy new gadget without reading the manual, right? This is your love manual, making sure everything runs smoothly, no matter what. A prenuptial agreement is your financial roadmap, protecting you and your partner as you embark on this incredible journey together. It is about love, trust, and smart planning. By understanding what a prenup is and what it aims to achieve, you are setting yourselves up for a future that is secure, happy, and filled with love.

***

Types of Property

Let's talk about prenup language and a little bit of family law so you can follow the significance of prenup terms and your financial decisions contained within.
There are three types of property: separate, marital, and community. Understanding these terms is crucial because they help define what belongs to whom in the eyes of the law. When you are creating your prenup, you will decide how to categorize different types of property, which can make a huge difference if you ever need to divide your assets.

Separate Property: Keeping What's Yours

Separate property is the property that belongs to one spouse individually. It includes assets acquired before the marriage, inheritances, gifts specifically given to one spouse, and anything specified as separate in the prenup. For example, Sheldon's comic book collection, which he had before marrying Amy, remains his separate property.

Examples of Separate Property:
- Assets you owned before getting married
- Gifts and inheritances given specifically to you during the marriage
- Personal injury settlements paid to you

Prenup Example: In their prenup, Emily and Richard agree that Emily's grandma's ring, given to her before the wedding, remains as Emily's separate property.

Marital Property: What You Build Together

Marital property is property acquired during the marriage, regardless of who paid for it. It includes a joint bank account, furniture purchased for the house, and even investments made, as long as these purchases were made after the couple got married. For example, the cozy little house Penny and Leonard bought together after tying the knot is considered marital property.

Examples of Marital Property:
- Income earned by either spouse during the marriage
- Property purchased with that income
- Joint bank accounts

Prenup Example: Lorelai and Luke decide that the home they buy together after getting married will be considered marital property, even though Luke is providing the money for their down payment.

Community Property: Equal Shares in Certain States

This term is relevant in states with community property laws (like California and Texas). It means all property acquired during the marriage is owned equally by both spouses.

Community Property Example: Howard and Bernadette live in a community property state, like California, so the money either of them earn during the marriage and any property they buy with that money are split 50/50.

"Community property" is a term relevant in states with specific community property laws, like California or Texas. Not every state is considered a "community property state." If a couple lives in a community property state, the law automatically assumes that everything each of them acquires during the marriage is owned equally by both. But even in these states, a prenup can override the default rules and specify how you want things handled.

Community Property States:
Arizona, California, Idaho, Louisiana, Nevada, New Mexico, Texas, Washington, and Wisconsin.

Prenup Example: Even though they now live in California, a community property state, Rory and Logan's prenup specifies that Logan's business income remains his separate property. (Team Logan! In my alternate ending, they are together and happy, no matter what state they live in.)

***

Historical Context: The evolution of prenuptial agreements and their legal significance over time.

Look, I'm going to go ahead and warn you, this section is a little background on the history of prenups. If you do not care about how it used to be and only care about how it is today ... Go ahead and skip to Chapter Two. Trust me, no hard feelings!

Still here? Okay, get ready for a little history lesson. Don't worry, it will be a quick backstory of prenups. You might be surprised to learn that prenups have been around for a long time—way before modern celebrity gossip made them famous! Did you know that one of the earliest recorded prenups dates back to 2,000 BCE in ancient Mesopotamia? That's right, prenups have been around for nearly 4,000 years! It just goes to show that the idea of planning for the future is as old as time itself.

Once Upon a Time...

Believe it or not, prenups are not some newfangled concept cooked up by Hollywood lawyers. These nifty agreements have roots that go way back. Picture ancient Egypt, where marriage contracts were all the rage. Yep, even the pharaohs were making sure their gold was properly sorted out. These contracts were all about protecting family assets and making sure everyone knew what was what.

Flash forward to ancient Greece and Rome, where dowries (money or property brought by a bride to her husband) were a big deal. Early prenup-like agreements helped ensure that dowries were handled properly and returned to the bride's family if things did not work out.

Moving up to medieval Europe: Imagine knights in shining armor, grand castles, and ... prenups? Absolutely! During this time, marriage was often about strategic alliances and property. Prenups helped to ensure that land and wealth stayed within families, protecting noble lineages and securing political alliances. Romantic, right?

As we move into the Renaissance, marriage agreements continued to evolve. During this cultural explosion of art and knowledge, people were still pretty savvy about their finances. Prenups (or marriage contracts) became more detailed and sophisticated, outlining dowries, inheritance rights, and property divisions. They were all about ensuring that everyone's interests were protected, which just goes to show that love and practicality have always gone hand in hand.

Jumping ahead to the 19th and 20th centuries, we see prenuptial agreements starting to look more like what we are familiar with today. As women gained more legal rights and the concept of marriage shifted from economic necessity to romantic partnership, prenups adapted to these changes. They began to focus more on individual property rights and financial arrangements, reflecting the growing importance of personal agency in marriage.

Welcome to the present day, where prenups are more relevant than ever. With people marrying later in life, often after establishing careers and accumulating assets, prenups have become a smart way to protect both partners' interests. Today's prenups cover everything from property division to spousal support, debt responsibility, and even pet custody (because, let's be honest, fur babies are family too!).

Why It Matters

So, why is all this history important? Understanding the evolution of prenups helps us see their enduring value. Prenups have always been about protecting what matters most, whether it is land, gold, or your cherished comic book collection. They are a testament to the importance of planning and fairness in relationships, and they illustrate that planning for the future is a timeless act of love.

Legally, prenups hold significant weight. They provide a clear framework for handling finances and assets, reducing the potential for conflict if things do not go as planned. By setting expectations and outlining responsibilities, prenups help ensure that both partners enter marriage with eyes wide open, ready for whatever the future holds.

The next time that someone says prenups are unromantic or unnecessary, you do not have to believe them. Prenups have evolved with the times, adapting to the changing landscape of love and partnership. Your prenup will be special because it will be made specifically for you and your partnership.

Chapter 2

Money, Money, Money: Financial Transparency and Communication

Like ABBA said, let's talk Money, Money, Money. Financial transparency and communication. I know, I know ... talking about money can be a bit like trying to eat soup with a fork–awkward and messy. But fear not! With a little guidance, we are going to make this process smooth and pain free.

Let's get something straight: a prenup is not just a legal document. It is a golden opportunity to have those all-important money talks. Think of it as financial therapy, where you both lay your cards on the table and start building a solid financial foundation for your future together.

Picture this: You're a few months into your marriage, and suddenly, you discover that your partner has a mountain of student loans or a secret credit card debt. Yikes! By discussing your finances upfront in a prenup and disclosing your assets and debts, you avoid these nasty surprises. Everything is out in the open from the get-go. This transparency means fewer shocks down the road and sets the stage for honest communication about money. You both can know exactly what you are getting into by joining lives and can be prepared to tackle any existing debt together. With the peace of mind that disclosing finances brings, you can sleep better knowing that you do not have skeletons in the financial closet.

Tackling your financial future together builds trust and fosters teamwork. When you are both involved in planning and managing your finances, it reinforces that you are in this together. A prenup helps you start those conversations and makes sure you are both on the same page.

***

Why Talking About Finances with Your Partner is Awesome:

Collaboration: You're working together towards common goals.

Trust: Financial transparency builds a stronger foundation of trust.

Support: You've got each other's backs, no matter what financial hurdles come your way.

Example: Lily and Marshall use their prenup discussions to set joint savings goals for their future vacations and paying off Lily's credit card debt. They even decide on a fun monthly "financial date night" to review their budget and celebrate their progress.

Knowing each other's financial situation means you can set realistic, achievable goals. Want to buy a house, travel the world, or start a business? These discussions help you map out how to get there, step by step. Together, set goals that are both ambitious and achievable. You are in a relationship and are both invested in a shared vision for your future. Make the journey more rewarding from the beginning

Example: Bella and Edward dream of opening a vegetarian restaurant together. During their prenup discussions, they outline a savings plan and timeline to make this dream a reality. They also agree on how to handle financial responsibilities if the business faces tough times.

A prenup is not just about protecting assets or planning for the worst. It is about creating a solid foundation for your financial future together. It is about teamwork, transparency, and setting goals that bring you closer as a couple. So, embrace this opportunity to have those crucial money talks, and watch your relationship grow stronger and your dreams become reality.

***

Conversation Starters with Your Partner

Okay, so how do you kick off these money talks without it feeling like a trip to the dentist? Here are some icebreakers to get the conversation flowing:

- **Start with something fun**: "What's your dream vacation?" or "Where do you see us in five years financially?" This helps ease into the more serious stuff.

- **Spill the beans**: Share a money secret, like "I have a habit of buying too many shoes" or "I'm actually a budgeting wizard." This can make the conversation more easy-going and less intimidating by getting it all out there.

- **Goal setting**: Ask, "What are our top financial goals as a couple?" This shifts the focus from individual finances to your shared future.

- **Or, make it a game:** Everyone likes games! Pop open a bottle of wine or crack open some bourbon. Every time one of you says "assets," drink! Every time one of you says "debt," give each other a smooch! Or use deserts instead of drinks. That actually sounds delightful!

Approach these conversations with a positive attitude and a sense of teamwork. Celebrate small victories, like paying off a debt or reaching a savings milestone. Remember, the goal is to strengthen your relationship and build a secure future together. It is not about one partner being on trial for their spending habits. Discussing your financials is about the two of you, your prenup is about the two of you, and your marriage is about the two of you.

More Tips for Fun Financial Talks:

- **Financial Date Nights**: Make a regular date night to review your finances. Order takeout, open a bottle of wine, and make it an enjoyable experience.

- **Celebrate Wins**: Whenever you hit a financial goal, celebrate it! Treat yourselves to something special: champagne toast, ice cream date, or a movie night.

- **Stay Positive**: Focus on your shared goals and the progress you are making together.

***

The Types of Financial Disclosures and Information You Need to Share

Now, let's get down to brass tacks. Here is what you need to put on the table:

1. **Assets**: List out all your assets—savings, property, retirement account, investments, that secret stash of cash in your sock drawer. Transparency is key!

2. **Debts**: Be honest about any debts you are bringing into the marriage. This includes student loans, credit card balances, and that car loan you would rather forget about.

3. **Income**: Share your income details. This is not about who makes more; it is about understanding your combined financial power.

4. **Expenses**: Discuss your regular expenses and spending habits. Are you a saver or a spender? Knowing this helps you plan a budget that works for both of you.

5. **Future Plans**: Talk about your financial goals and plans. Do you want to buy a house? Have kids? Travel? Knowing this helps you align your financial strategy.

What do you actually need to talk about when it comes to setting financial expectations, and talking about Money, Money, Money? Here are some key areas to focus on:

Income: Who is Bringing in the Bacon?

This is where you get real about how much money is coming into your household. Whether you are both working full-time, one of you is freelancing, or maybe someone's staying home to take care of the kids—lay it all out on the table. Who is bringing in the bacon, and how much is there?

Is one of you earning significantly more than the other? Or maybe you are both contributing equally? It is important to discuss how you feel about the income balance and how it might affect your financial decisions. If one of you is the primary breadwinner, does that come with certain expectations or responsibilities? And if so, how do you both feel about that?

Talking about income is not just about numbers; it is about understanding the dynamics of your financial partnership. It is also about being honest with each other about your career goals and how they might impact your income over time. Maybe one of you is planning to go back to school, or perhaps there is a big promotion on the horizon. Whatever the case, keeping the lines of communication open about your income will help you both feel more secure and aligned as a team.

Expenses: Where is That Bacon Going?

Now that you have figured out who is bringing in the bacon, it is time to talk about where that bacon is going. We all have expenses, and some are more fun to talk about than others. Rent or mortgage payments, utilities, groceries, car payments, insurance, student loans, the list goes on. And do not forget the little things that can add up like Netflix subscriptions, gym memberships, your daily coffee run....

Start by listing out all your fixed expenses. These are the bills that come like clockwork every month, including things like housing, utilities, car payments, and insurance. These are the non-negotiables that you have got to cover, no matter what.

Next, take a look at your variable expenses. This is the stuff that can change from month to month. These could include groceries, the Hulu account, dining out, entertainment, and shopping. These are the areas where you might have a bit more flexibility, but they can also be the sneaky budget busters if you are not careful.

The goal here is to get a clear picture of where your money is going each month. Are you both comfortable with how much is being spent on certain things? Are there areas where you would like to cut back or save more? Maybe you want to save up for a big vacation or put more money into your retirement accounts. Or perhaps you have got your eye on that dream home and need to start saving for a down payment.

By having an open conversation about your expenses, you can make sure you are both on the same page about your spending priorities. You might even find that you have different spending styles. Maybe one of you is a saver and the other is a spender. If that's the case, it is important to find a balance that works for both of you.

***

Budgeting as a Team

Once you have laid out your income and expenses, the next step is to create a budget that works for both of you. This is not about being restrictive or controlling, but is about making sure you are both on track to meet your financial goals. Maybe you want to pay off debt, save for a house, or start a family. Whatever your goals are, a budget will help you get there. Budgeting as a team is also a great way to build trust and strengthen your relationship. It shows that you are both committed to working together towards a shared financial future.

1. **Saving Goals**: Are you saving for a house, retirement, a vacation, or maybe just a rainy day? Set clear goals so you can both work towards them.

Retirement conversations open a lot of doors. First, when do you both want or plan to retire? What strategy do you both have to achieve certain retirement goals? Do you want to live more frugally so you can retire early? Do you want to live a full and vibrant life and work longer so you enjoy both your working life and retirement life? What type of retirement lifestyle do you have in mind? Traveling for a year? Living and staying close to home and living a more humble lifestyle? These are just a few of the many questions you need to dive into with your partner to make sure you are on the same page about both saving and spending to create the retirement plan of your dreams ... And as of right now, you could have very different retirement dreams. Go ahead and find out how you will work together to compromise and work together toward your goals.

Do you (both) want to build a passive income empire? It is many peoples' dreams to have their money work for them while they sleep (talk about sweet dreams, eh?). I'm right there with you, but that opens the door to yet another multitude of questions. How do you build this empire? Strategy and aggressive investment strategies? Cryptocurrency? Stocks? NFTs? What about building a real estate empire? There are thousands of strategies to create passive income. Some require a large amount of capital to start, some are inherited, and some are built in blood, sweat, and tears. Some require a LOT of hard work and hands-on contributions, while others are more automated. Are you and your partner on the same page? Do you both value building your passive income portfolio to the same degree? Are you both willing to take risks? Are you both willing to invest time, energy, and money?

Let's talk about fun purchases! Do you want a Birkin bag? A yacht? Regular Botox injections? The latest and greatest golf clubs? A country club membership? The new (and incredibly ugly, no offense) Tesla truck? A ski trip in Aspen and a trip to the Maldives every year? These are all things that most people need to save and plan for (if you are in a tax bracket where you can make these purchases on a whim, congrats! But you can skip this section), meaning as a couple you need to determine saving goals for big ticket items and make sure you both value the purchase to the same degree.

2. **Debt Management**: So, here is the deal: debt is not exactly a sexy topic, but it is one of those things you *have* to talk about before you tie the knot. Think of it as the financial equivalent of "What's your biggest pet peeve?" You might not want to know, but you *need* to know. (What is worse: They chew with their mouth open, or they have a bunch of secret debt?)

Start by asking each other, "Do either of us have debts?" This could include student loans, credit card balances, car loans, or even that random store credit card you opened just to get 10% off a new couch. Getting all those numbers out in the open helps prevent any financial curveballs down the road.

Once you know what you are dealing with, the next step is to figure out how you are going to tackle it. Will you combine forces to pay off the debt faster? Or will each of you handle your own pre-existing debts? Discuss how you will manage any new debt you might take on together. Maybe you are planning to buy a house or start a business—these things can lead to shared debt, so it is important to be on the same page. The last thing you want is to feel blindsided by a big, scary debt monster hiding underneath the marital bed.

3. **Spending Habits**: Are you a saver or a spender, what about your partner? Understanding each other's

spending habits can prevent a lot of arguments down the road.

Are you a "Let's save every penny for a rainy day" kind of person, or are you more of a "You only live once, let's buy that new gadget" type? Neither approach is wrong, but it can cause some friction if you are not on the same page.

Take the time to understand each other's spending habits. If one of you is a spender and the other is a saver, it is important to acknowledge those differences and figure out a way to balance them. You might need to set some ground rules—like agreeing on a monthly budget or setting limits on discretionary spending.

By having this conversation, you can prevent a lot of arguments down the road. No one wants to get into a heated discussion over why someone bought *another* pair of Manolos when you are supposed to be saving for a down payment on a house. (Not everyone is blessed with a rent control apartment in Manhattan, Carrie.) Trust me, understanding each other's spending style is key to avoiding financial friction.

4. **Emergency Fund**: Ah, the emergency fund—your financial life preserver for when life decides to throw a storm your way. It is not a matter of *if* something unexpected will happen, but *when*. So, how much do you need in your emergency fund? And how are you going to build it?

The general rule of thumb is to have three to six months' worth of living expenses saved up, but this can vary depending on your situation. Maybe you are both in stable jobs and feel comfortable with a smaller cushion, or maybe one of you is self-employed and needs a bit more of a buffer.

Once you have agreed on the amount, you need to figure out how to build it. Will you both contribute equally? Or will you allocate a percentage of your income? And where will you keep this emergency fund? In a high-yield savings account, under the mattress, or somewhere in between? This conversation is crucial because an emergency fund is not just about the money, but is about peace of mind. It is knowing that if the car breaks down, the roof starts leaking, or one of you loses your job, you have got a financial cushion to fall back on. And when you have got that safety net in place, you can both sleep a little easier at night, knowing you are prepared for whatever life throws your way.

***

Types of Financial Arrangements Couples Can Use

Alright, now that we've covered the basics, let's talk about different financial arrangements you can set up. Here are a few examples:

1. **Joint Accounts**: You pool all your money into one account. This can be great for simplicity and fostering a sense of teamwork, but it requires a lot of trust and communication.

Example*: Jointly Under The Sea*

After overcoming the battle with the Sea Witch, Eric and Ariel are thrilled to get married! After getting engaged, they sat down for one of those big "money talks" that everyone says is so important. You know, the kind where you have to be honest about everything—from your savings account to that secret shoe fund (Come on, the girl just got legs. Give her a break).

Eric, being a numbers guy (and concerned about the kingdom), was all about the idea of simplicity. "Why not just put all our money into one account?" he suggested one evening while they were cooking dinner together. "It'll make things so much easier. One account, one budget, and no confusion about who's paying for what."

Ariel, on the other hand, was a little more cautious. She liked the idea of teamwork, but the thought of merging their finances completely made her a bit nervous. "But what if I want to buy something without feeling like I need to ask permission?" she asked, brushing her hair (with a dinglehopper) while trying not to sound too worried.

Eric smiled and reassured her, "It is not about permission, it is about trust. We would both have access to the account, and we would still have our own spending money. We would just be working together to manage the big stuff, like bills and savings."

After a bit more discussion, they decided to give the joint account a try. They opened a joint checking account where both of their paychecks would be deposited, and they agreed on a budget for their shared expenses like rent, groceries, and utilities. They also set up an additional savings account for their future goals, like buying a house or taking a cruise.

At first, it was a little tricky. There were a few moments where Ariel felt like she had to justify every purchase—like the time she bought a new pair of shoes and a gizmo, so Eric asked, "Do we really *need* that right now?" But after some honest conversations, they found a rhythm that worked for them. They set aside a small amount of "fun money" each month for each of them to spend however they liked, no questions asked. That way, they both had a bit of financial freedom while still working together on the bigger picture goals.

As time went on, they found that having a joint account actually brought them closer. They were more aware of each other's financial habits, and they started to see their money as a shared resource rather than something that belonged to one of them individually. It was not always perfect, and they had to keep communicating to make sure they were on the same page. But overall, the joint account helped them feel more like a team, working together towards their shared goals.

So, if you are considering a joint account like Eric and Ariel, remember that it is all about trust, communication, and a bit of flexibility. It can be a great way to simplify your finances and build a stronger financial partnership, but only if you are both comfortable with the arrangement.

2. **Separate Accounts**: You each keep your own money and divide shared expenses. This can work well if you have different spending habits or financial goals.

Example: *Separate Offices?*

Jim and Pam have been together for a few years, and they are finally taking the plunge into marriage. They are a great match—Jim's the laid-back, funny guy who always has a prank up his sleeve, and Pam's the creative, organized one who keeps everything running smoothly. But when it comes to money, they have realized they have different approaches....

One evening, they are sitting on the couch, talking about how they are going to handle their finances after they get married. "So, how do you feel about a joint account?" Jim asks, trying to gauge Pam's thoughts.

Pam thinks for a moment. "I'm not sure a joint account is the best fit for us," she says. "I mean, you know how I love to budget every penny, and you are more of a 'live in the moment' kind of guy."

Jim chuckles. "Yeah, I guess I do tend to splurge on things like new tech gadgets or spontaneous weekend getaways. But I love how you keep us grounded with your budgeting."

Pam smiles. "Exactly. And I do not want us to argue about money just because we have different spending habits. What if we each kept our own accounts and just split the shared expenses?"

Jim raises an eyebrow. "Like, I pay for some things, and you pay for others?"

"Kind of," Pam explains. "We would keep our own accounts, so you can buy whatever gadgets you want, and I can keep saving for that art retreat I have been dreaming about. But when it comes to shared expenses—like rent, utilities, groceries—we would split them down the middle."

Jim nods, starting to see the benefits. "So, we are still sharing the important stuff, but we each get to manage our own money our own way. That could work."

Pam continues, "Plus, it is a good way to respect each other's financial goals. I know you want to have fun with your money, and I want to save for specific things. This way, we do not have to compromise on our individual priorities."

Jim grins. "I like it. But how do we keep track of who's paying for what?"

Pam pulls out her phone and shows Jim a budgeting app. "We can use this to track our shared expenses. We just input what we've paid for, and it keeps a running total. At the end of the month, we settle up if there is any difference."

Jim looks impressed. "You've really thought this through, haven't you?"

Pam laughs. "You know me—I love a good plan. But I think this arrangement gives us the best of both worlds. We're still a team, but we get to keep our financial independence."

Jim leans back on the couch, feeling relieved. "I'm all for it. I think this could be the perfect setup for us."

So, Jim and Pam decide to go with separate accounts. They each keep their own money, but they have got a plan for handling shared expenses. Over the next few months, they find that it works well for them. Jim enjoys his tech splurges without worrying about affecting their overall budget, and Pam happily saves for her art retreat.

They still have to communicate about their shared expenses, but it is more of a check-in than a negotiation. Because they respect each other's financial independence, they find that money is one less thing to argue about.

In the end, Jim and Pam's decision to keep separate accounts helps them maintain their individuality while still working together as a couple. It is a financial arrangement that fits their unique relationship, and it is one more reason they are such a great match.

3. **Hybrid Approach**: A mix of joint and separate accounts. For example, you might have a joint account for household expenses and separate accounts for personal spending. Best of both worlds! This is my personal favorite. Think about it, what if you want to buy your love a surprise? Well, it is a lot easier if they cannot see it on the bank statement!

Example: A Hybrid Game of Thrones

In a world where dragons soar and the Iron Throne awaits, even royalty like Daenerys Targaryen and Jon Snow have to figure out how to manage their finances. After all, ruling the Seven Kingdoms is expensive business, and even queens and kings have bills to pay.

One evening, after a long day of dragon rides and council meetings, Daenerys and Jon sit down by the fire in their cozy castle quarters to discuss their finances. "We need to talk about how we are going to manage our money now that we are, well, ruling together," Daenerys begins, looking thoughtful.

Jon, ever the practical Northerner, nods. "Aye, it is important. But we do not exactly have the same approach to spending."

Daenerys smiles. "Exactly. I'm more of a 'let's rebuild the world' kind of spender, and you are ... well, you are a little more conservative."

Jon smirks. "I suppose you could say that. So, what do you suggest?"

Daenerys leans forward, excited to share her idea. "How about a hybrid approach? We could have a joint account for all our shared expenses—like castle upkeep, feeding the dragons, paying the Unsullied—and then we keep separate accounts for personal spending."

Jon raises an eyebrow, intrigued. "How would that work?"

Daenerys explains, "The joint account would cover all the household and ruling expenses—things we both contribute to and benefit from. But with our separate accounts, we would have the freedom to spend on whatever we want without having to consult the other person. For instance, if I wanted to buy you a surprise gift or, say, fund a little expedition to explore beyond the Wall, you would not see it on our joint bank statement."

Jon grins. "I like that idea. It is the best of both worlds. We're working together on the important stuff, but we still have a bit of independence."

Daenerys nods. "Exactly. Plus, it makes things easier when it comes to managing our personal spending. If you want to invest in some new armor or I want to buy another dragon egg, we do not have to justify it to each other."

Jon chuckles. "And what about when it comes to saving?"

Daenerys thinks for a moment. "We could agree on a set amount to contribute to savings from our joint account. That way, we are both building our future together, but we still have room for personal savings in our separate accounts."

Jon leans back, clearly impressed. "You've really thought this through. I think this could work."

Daenerys smiles, relieved that Jon's on board. "It is a way to make sure we are both happy and that money does not become a point of tension. We've got enough battles to fight without having to worry about that."

And so, Daenerys and Jon Snow adopt the hybrid financial approach. They set up a joint account for all their shared expenses and responsibilities, while keeping separate accounts for their personal spending. This arrangement allows them to work together as a team while maintaining their individuality—a balance that proves invaluable as they continue to rule the Seven Kingdoms.

Over time, they find that this approach works perfectly for them. Daenerys enjoys the freedom to pursue her grand visions, while Jon appreciates having the ability to manage his own spending without any pressure. And best of all, when Daenerys surprises Jon with a rare Valyrian steel dagger, he's genuinely surprised—because he never saw it coming on the bank statement.

In the end, the hybrid approach helps Daenerys and Jon manage their finances in a way that suits their unique personalities and strengthens their bond as both rulers and partners. It is a financial strategy fit for a king and queen, and one that helps them navigate the challenges of ruling with both wisdom and love.

Each approach has its pros and cons, so it is all about finding what works best for you as a couple. There is no one-size-fits-all here, just what makes you both comfortable and happy.

**

Using the Prenup Goals Worksheet

To make all this easier, we've got a handy-dandy **Prenup Goals Worksheet** located in Appendix A. It will guide you through all the important topics. Here is how to use it:

- **Fill It Out Together**: Sit down with your partner and fill out the worksheet together. Make it a date night—order some takeout, pour a glass of wine, and get to work.

- **Be Honest**: This is your chance to be completely transparent. The more honest you are, the stronger your financial foundation will be.

- **Discuss and Adjust**: Use the worksheet to spark discussions. If you have different views on spending or saving, talk it out and find a middle ground.

- **Plan for the Future**: Use the information to set financial goals and create a plan that works for both of you.

So, there you have it! Setting financial expectations and having open, honest discussions about money is crucial for a strong and happy marriage. It might seem daunting at first, but with a little humor, some great conversation starters, and our handy Prenup Goals Worksheet, you will be pros in no time.

Remember, this is all about building a solid foundation for your future together. By being transparent and clear about your financial expectations, you are setting yourselves up for success. Cheers to financial clarity and a bright, beautiful future!

Chapter 3

Safeguard your Separate Property ... Or Don't!

One potential use of prenups is to keep your separate property safe. If you need a refresher on what separate property is (or if you skipped it before because it sounded boring), please refer to page 17. Whether you have got a killer kaleidoscope collection, a family heirloom, or a business you have built from the ground up, you might want to keep those things safe and sound as just your own. Or maybe you are totally fine with sharing everything and rolling with the punches. Either way, you should chat about all your options with your partner!

Before we dive into the various separate properties you can bring into a marriage, let's break down the three most common ways to define your premarital separate assets going into your marriage. Keep in mind that you can define different properties under these different approaches, or you can have all assets treated the same way under one of these approaches. Remember, it is *your* prenup, done *your* way.

Approach #1: The Traceable Option - Separate Property Remains Separate.

Under this approach, all premarital assets and any property traceable to those assets remain separate property. Meaning, all increases in value or any new assets exchanged or acquired with the premarital assets will remain separate property during the marriage. Basically, that is a fancy way of saying, "What's mine stays mine, and what's yours stays yours, plus any extras that come from those things."

Here is how it works: Imagine you have a savings account, a car, and maybe even a little plot of land that you owned before you got hitched. With The Traceable Option, all of that stuff remains yours, even after you say, "I do." But it does not stop there. If those assets increase in value or you swap them for something new, those new or improved assets *still belong to you*. Let's break it down:

- **Premarital Assets**: These are the things you own before you walk down the aisle. It could be a savings account you have been building since your first job, a house you bought on your own, or that vintage guitar collection you have been obsessively curating. Under

The Traceable Option, these stay as your separate property, safe from the mingling of marital assets.

- **Traceable to Premarital Assets**: Now, let's say your savings account earns interest, or you sell that plot of land and buy a cozy cabin in the mountains. Any increase in value or new assets you acquire by selling or trading your premarital property remain yours. The key here is that these new or improved assets can be directly traced back to your original premarital property.

- **During the Marriage**: Even after you tie the knot, if you use your premarital assets to buy something new— like upgrading that vintage car with a shiny new paint job—it is still considered separate property, as long as you can trace it back to your original premarital asset.

But remember, the key to this approach is keeping everything traceable. If you start mixing these assets with marital property—like using that savings account to fund a joint vacation or putting your spouse's name on the title of your premarital house—it might blur the lines. Trust me, keeping things clear will save you from plenty of headaches later on.

Why Choose the Traceable Option?

The Traceable Option is perfect for those who want to protect their premarital property while allowing it to grow and evolve without losing ownership. It is a way to ensure that what you brought into the marriage remains yours, even as life changes and assets shift. Plus, it gives you peace of mind knowing that your hard-earned assets will not automatically become joint property just because you are now sharing your life with someone else. In a nutshell, The

Traceable Option is all about keeping things clear, clean, and, well, traceable. It is like putting your premarital property in a protective bubble, where it can grow and thrive, but still belongs to you.

Approach #2: The All-In Approach - It's All Property

Under this approach, all premarital assets will be considered marital or community property. This is the ultimate "what's mine is yours" strategy.

Here is how it works: With the All-In Approach, every single thing you owned before saying "I do" gets thrown into the marital pot. Yep, that means all your premarital assets—your savings, your car, that vintage record collection—instantly become joint property the moment you get married. Let's break it down:

- **Premarital Assets**: These are the things you brought into the marriage, like your savings account, your house, or that prized comic book collection. Under this approach, the moment you are married, these assets are no longer just yours—they are shared with your spouse.

- **Marital or Community Property**: Once your premarital assets are in the marital pot, they are considered marital property or community property, depending on what state you live in. That means both you and your spouse have equal ownership and say over them. Whether it is selling the house, spending the savings, or deciding what to do with that record collection—it is all done together.

- **During the Marriage**: Throughout your marriage, all the assets you brought in and any new ones you acquire will be considered joint property. So, when you sell that premarital house or cash in on your old savings bonds, the proceeds are split between you and your spouse.

Why Choose the All-In Approach?

The All-In Approach is for couples who are ready to go all in—no holding back. It is about fully merging your lives, including your finances, from day one. This approach is perfect for those who see marriage as the ultimate partnership, where everything is shared equally, and there is no need to draw lines between what's mine and what's yours.

In a nutshell, The All-In Approach is the ultimate expression of financial unity. It is about starting your marriage with a clean slate, where everything you brought into the relationship and everything you build together becomes part of your shared journey.

Approach #3: The Hybrid Approach or Shared Option

Under this approach, all premarital assets will remain separate property; however, any increases in value or any new assets that are exchanged for or acquired with the premarital assets will become marital or community property. Essentially, "What's mine is mine, but any growth or new goodies we get from it, we share."

Here is the deal: With The Shared Option, all the stuff you brought into the marriage—like your savings, your car, or that plot of land—stays yours, nice and safe. However, here is the twist: if that stuff increases in value or you trade it in for something new, the gains or new assets are not just yours anymore—they are part of your shared marital or community property.

Let's break it down:

- **Premarital Assets**: Just like in The Traceable Option, these are the things you own before you tie the knot. They start off as your separate property, meaning they belong only to you.

- **Increases in Value or New Assets**: Here is where The Shared Option takes a different path. If your premarital assets grow—like if your savings earn interest, your plot of land skyrockets in value, or you swap your old car for a snazzy new one—that growth or those new assets are considered marital or community property. In other words, they belong to both you and your spouse.

- **During the Marriage**: As life goes on and your premarital assets evolve, anything that comes from them gets shared. So, if you sell your premarital house and buy a new one with your spouse, that new house is something you both own together.

Why Choose The Shared Option?

The Shared Option is perfect for couples who want to keep their original premarital assets separate but are open to sharing the benefits and growth that come from them. It is a way to recognize that while you both came into the marriage with your own stuff, you are now building a life together and sharing in the rewards. It is like saying, "I brought this into the marriage, but I'm happy to share what it becomes with you."

In essence, The Shared Option is all about starting with what's yours and then growing together as a team. It is a way to protect your premarital assets while still embracing the idea that marriage is about sharing the ups and downs—and the financial growth that comes along the way.

***

Personal and Family Wealth: Safeguarding Assets Acquired Before Marriage

So, you have worked hard and built up some assets before saying "I do." Maybe it is a sweet condo, a vintage car, valuable snow globe collection, or a hefty savings account. How do you make sure these remain yours if things go sideways?

- **Identify Your Assets**: Start by listing everything you own that you *want* to keep separate. This includes property, bank accounts, investments, and yes, even that rare Pokémon card collection.

- **Get It in Writing**: A prenup can spell out what stays yours no matter what. It is like putting a "Hands Off" sign on your stuff, legally speaking.

- **Keep It Separate OR Don't**: To make sure your pre-marriage assets remain yours, avoid commingling them with marital assets. For example, do not use your premarital savings to buy a joint property, unless your prenup specifically addresses the scenario and carves out alternative rules. Or use The All-In Approach.

**

Business Ownership: Protecting Your Entrepreneurial Baby

Got a business? Awesome! Whether it is a thriving tech startup or a cozy little bakery, you will want to make sure it is protected. I cannot tell you the times I have had a D-word (divorce) client who started a wildly successful business during the marriage and cannot wrap their brain around having to split the business or payout half the value of their business to their ex. Depending on where you live, you could lose half under the state-created prenup. Yikes. On the other hand, maybe your spouse does not work during the creation and nurturing of the business and raises the children to allow the business-minded spouse to succeed. You may want your prenup to give the non-working spouse a percentage of the business to compensate for their personal sacrifice and contribution that allowed you to create the successful business. Or maybe together you decide on a completely unique and innovative way to split the business upon the event of death or divorce. It really is up to you!

Example: *A Wolf's Business in a Prenup*

Let's take a little trip to Wall Street and talk about our friends Jordan and Naomi. You know, the power couple who seemed to have it all: the mansion, the yacht, and yes, Jordan's wildly successful business. For purposes of this story, just go with this deviation from the plot line and do not get your panties in a wad on the accuracy. Jordan started his company during their marriage, pouring blood, sweat, and maybe a few too many questionable decisions into building his empire. Meanwhile, Naomi was holding down the fort at home, raising the kids, and making sure everything ran smoothly on the home front. Teamwork, right?

But here is the thing—when it all went south, Jordan was floored by the idea that half of his business could be Naomi's. He was the one closing deals, making calls, and staying up all night to keep the business afloat. How could she get half? Well, depending on where you live, that's exactly what can happen under the state's default laws—like a state-created prenup that you did not even know you signed up for. Without proper planning, the court might decide that Naomi, who supported the household, deserves half of the business Jordan built. And, that might be fair, given how much she sacrificed to make his success possible. But would it not have been better if they had spelled it all out from the start?

Spell It Out in the Prenup:
First things first, if you are Jordan—or Naomi—you will want to make sure your business is protected in your prenup. If you are the one who started the business, you might decide that it should remain your separate property. That means that no matter how successful it becomes, it is yours and yours alone. Or maybe you are more of a team player, and you opt for The All-In Approach, where both of you share everything, including the business. Whatever you decide, make sure it is crystal clear in the prenup.

Valuation Clause:

Now, let's talk about the value of that business. Imagine this: Jordan and Naomi split up (bummer, I know), and suddenly they are arguing over how much the business is worth. Is it worth a cool million? Ten million? More? Disputes over business valuation can get ugly and expensive. Just think about how much time and money they will spend just trying to agree on a number. That is where a valuation clause comes in handy. By including this in the prenup, you can outline exactly how the business will be valued if things do not work out. Maybe you agree to have it valued by an independent expert, or you set a specific formula. Whatever the method, it saves a ton of headaches later on.

Salary and Contributions:

But what if Naomi wasn't just at home? What if she was right there in the trenches with Jordan, working in the business? In that case, it is super important to decide whether she will get a salary for her work or if her contributions mean she gets a stake in the business. Let's say Naomi was handling all the marketing, keeping the clients happy, and basically running the show behind the scenes. Should she not get a piece of the pie? That is a conversation that should happen before things get complicated, and the prenup is the perfect place to make those decisions.

An Innovative Twist:

Finally, let's not forget that you do not have to follow any set rules. You can get creative with your prenup! Maybe Jordan and Naomi decide on a completely unique way to handle the business if things go south. Maybe they agree that Naomi gets a percentage of the business based on the number of years they are married, or they set up a trust for the kids that kicks in only if the business hits a certain value. The beauty of a prenup is that it is your document, and you can make it work however you want.

The Bottom Line:
In the end, whether you are a Jordan, a Naomi, or just someone who's working hard to build something great, it is important to protect your business in your prenup. It is about more than just numbers. It is about making sure that both partners feel respected, valued, and secure. So take the time to talk it out, plan it out, and write it down. Your future self will thank you.

***

Inheritance and Heirlooms: Keeping Family Treasures in the Family

Family heirlooms and inheritance are special. They carry sentimental value and a sense of legacy. Let's make sure they stay in the family.

1. **List Your Heirlooms**: Make a list of all the items you have inherited or expect to inherit. Think Grandma's ring, your dad's antique watch, or that funky painting your great-aunt left you.

2. **State the Ownership**: Clearly state in your prenup that these items are yours alone. It is like saying, "This ring is not just a ring; it is a piece of my family history."

3. **Future Inheritances**: Consider including a clause about future inheritances to ensure they stay with you. Better safe than sorry!

***

Deciding to Whether to Separate or Share

Now, you might be thinking, "But we are in love! Sharing is caring!" And that is totally cool too. If you are comfortable mixing everything together, go for it! Just be clear about your choices:

1. **Joint Ownership**: If you decide to share your assets, make sure your prenup reflects this. It should outline how you will manage your combined wealth.

2. **Equal Partnership**: Emphasize that you see your marriage as an equal partnership, financially and otherwise. This sets the tone for mutual respect and cooperation.

***

Safeguarding your separate property (or choosing not to) is all about clear communication and smart planning. Whether it is personal wealth, a business, or family heirlooms, a prenup can help you protect what's important to you.

Remember, this is not about planning for the worst, it is about making sure both of you feel secure and respected in your relationship. Get that **Prenup Couples Quiz** located in Appendix B, have a fun and honest chat with your partner, and make some decisions that work best for both of you.

Chapter 4

Let's Talk about Debt Baby, Let's Talk About You and Me

Salt-N-Pepa had it right, we have to talk about all the good things ... and the bad. We are tackling a topic that is about as fun as a surprise dentist appointment: debt. Do not fret, I'm here to make it as painless as possible. We will explore how a prenup can help protect you from debt drama and what that means for your credit scores and borrowing future.

Shielding from Debt: Protecting Your Financial Future

Alright, let's start with the basics. Imagine you are dating someone who is amazing but happens to have a mountain of student loans or credit card debt. How do you ensure you do not end up stuck with that debt if things go south? Here is where a prenup can help you out.

1. **Pre-Existing Debt**: A prenup can specify that any debt one partner brings into the marriage remains their responsibility alone. Think of it like a "do not touch" sign for that debt pile. It is about protecting you from inheriting someone else's financial mess.

2. **Future Debt**: What about debt that accumulates during the marriage? You can outline how new debts will be handled. For instance, if one partner takes out a loan for a new business venture, the prenup can clarify who is responsible for paying it back.

3. **Debt Division**: If debt becomes a joint responsibility, decide how you will divide it. Will you split it 50/50, or will it be based on income? This helps prevent disputes if things do not go as planned.

Remember, like with almost everything in your prenup, you can make your own rules. Maybe one partner has $200,000 in student loan debt but they went to law school or medical school, leading to their healthy student loan balance. That partner also has a much higher earning potential than the other partner who has zero student loan debt but has a much lower earning potential. Depending on how these partners choose to handle their income and earnings in the marriage will also influence how they choose to handle their debts as well. These two may want to put all their income and earnings together and also pay one partner's debt together as well. Or they can keep both their debts and their earnings separate. It is truly a custom plan based on each partner's wishes and financial goals.

***

Credit Scores and Future Borrowing: The Impact of Debt

Now, let's chat about credit scores. Imagine your credit score as your financial report card. A high score means you are doing great while a low score might make lenders go, "Uh-oh." Here is how debt affects it and what you can do about it:

1. **Impact of Debt on Credit Scores**: If your partner has significant debt, it could impact both of your credit scores if you decide to co-sign on loans or open joint accounts. Lenders look at your combined financial picture, so it is like a group project where everyone's grade affects the others. Because of this, you and your partner may want to delay joining certain finances and applying for loans together for big purchases early in the marriage. You can always change the arrangement and add your partner to the mortgage or deed at a later date. The important thing is to TALK ABOUT IT. Decide together what will work best for you as a married couple.

2. **Joint Borrowing**: Planning to buy a house or get a car loan together? Your credit scores will play a big role. If one partner has a less-than-stellar credit history, it could

mean higher interest rates or even trouble getting approved. A prenup does not fix credit scores, but it can help you understand and manage the potential impacts. It is all about communication.

3. **Protecting Your Score**: To keep your credit score shining bright, keep an eye on your joint accounts and debt. Pay off balances regularly and avoid taking on too much debt together.

If one partner comes into the marriage with a lesser score than the other, it is also time to discuss how you jointly want to increase your scores as a collaborative couple. Remember, this is financial therapy without the couch. It is time to talk out what strategies are best for your long-term success as a married couple.

**

Let's face it, debt does not have to be a dealbreaker or a secret that haunts your relationship. With a prenup, you can set clear boundaries and protect yourselves from financial surprises. It is all about having honest discussions and making smart decisions to keep your financial future secure.

So, grab that **Prenup Goals Worksheet** from Appendix B and sit down with your partner to talk about debt. Set up your financial game plan and make sure you are both on the same page. Remember, a little planning now can save you a lot of stress later.

Chapter 5

From Spats to Smiles

Time for some conflict resolution! That is right, let's get in front of potential issues before they even happen. Ever had one of those moments where you and your partner are bickering over who left the milk out, and suddenly it feels like World War III? Do not worry, we have all been there. But guess what? A prenup can be your secret weapon for turning those spats into smiles.

Preventing Future Disputes: How Prenups Can Minimize Conflicts

We get it, no one wants to imagine their relationship ending, but it is wise to prepare for all possibilities. A prenup is not just a legal document, it is like a relationship GPS that helps guide you through potential bumps in the road. Here is how it can help prevent future disputes:

- **Clear Guidelines**: A prenup sets out clear rules for what happens to your assets and debts if things do not work out. It is like having a pre-set menu for a fancy dinner—everything is planned, and you do not have to argue over the choices.

- **Defined Terms**: With a prenup, you have already agreed on how to handle property division, alimony, and other financial matters. This means fewer surprises and less room for disagreements later. It is like preemptively answering all the tricky questions, so you do not have to face them in the heat of the moment.

- **Less Drama**: Knowing that there is a plan in place can reduce the emotional stress and drama of a breakup. It is like having a fire drill before the real thing—you are prepared and ready to handle things calmly.

- **Focus on What Matters**: With a prenup in place, you can focus on maintaining a positive relationship and working through issues that matter more, like where to go for dinner or which movie to watch. It is about saving your energy for the fun stuff!

Peace of Mind: The Psychological Benefits of Knowing Both Parties Are Protected

Now, let's talk about the warm fuzzies that come with having a prenup. It is not just about the legal stuff. It is also about how it makes you feel.

- **Security Blanket**: A prenup acts like a financial security blanket. It is like knowing there is a safety net under you when you are walking a tightrope. It gives you peace of mind knowing that no matter what happens, both of you are protected.

- **Reduced Anxiety**: Having a prenup can reduce anxiety about the future. It is like having the GPS for your road trip—you know where you are going and what to expect, so you can relax and enjoy the journey.

- **Stronger Bond**: Discussing and agreeing on a prenup together can actually strengthen your bond. It is a chance to talk openly about your values and expectations. It is like having a deep, meaningful conversation while sipping coffee—it brings you closer.

- **Confidence in Your Relationship**: Knowing that you are both protected can give you confidence in your relationship. It is like having a sturdy bridge between you—strong and reliable, no matter what's on the other side.

So, there you have it! Conflict resolution does not have to be a scary, stressful process. With a prenup, you are setting yourself up for fewer disputes and more peace of mind. It is about having a plan in place that lets you focus on what really matters: your relationship, your happiness, and maybe even that delicious dessert you are planning to share.

Chapter 6

Love Each Other During Marriage and Beyond

Let's Talk About the Future. The responsibilities during marriage and beyond are only nuisances if you do not know how you are going to handle them. Whether you are navigating separation, divorce, or even the great beyond, having a prenup can be your trusty sidekick, helping you be safe and prepared no matter what life throws your way. (Maybe a prenup will not act exactly like Robin, but I do think Batman has lots of cool stuff he would want to define in a prenup.)

Responsibilities During the Marriage.

How do you combine incomes, pay bills, and tackle debt as a dynamic duo? Let's chat about some practical (and fun) ways to handle your money matters together. Ready to become financial rockstars? Let's do this!

Combining Incomes: Double the Fun, Double the Funds

Combining incomes can feel like hitting the jackpot. Suddenly, there is more cash flow! But it also means more responsibility. Here are a few examples of how you can approach it together:

1. **Joint Bank Accounts**: Many couples choose to combine their incomes into a joint account. It is like having a big pot where all your money goes, making it easier to pay bills and track expenses.

   Example: Martin and Caroline decided to merge their incomes into a joint account. They both deposit their entire paychecks into this account and use it for all household expenses. This way, they can see their total income and plan accordingly.

2. **Separate Accounts with a Shared Pot**: Some couples prefer to keep individual accounts but contribute a set amount to a joint account for shared expenses. It is like having your cake and eating it too—individual freedom and shared responsibility.

   Example: Mia and Tyler each keep their own accounts but transfer 60% of their income to a joint account.

This shared pot covers rent, groceries, and utilities, while their personal accounts handle individual expenses and splurges. One of the benefits of this approach is that they can use the separate 40% of their income however they want without having to explain. Think about if Tyler wants to buy Mia a surprise birthday present with some diamonds in it. He does not want the bank account to give him away!

3. **The Hybrid Approach**: Combine the best of both worlds! Keep separate accounts, a joint account for shared expenses, and maybe even a "fun money" account for shared adventures.

   Example: Ryan and Tish have their personal accounts, a joint account for bills, and a fun money account. They contribute a bit to the fun money account each month for date nights, vacations, and spontaneous fun.

Paying Bills: Sharing the Load
Paying bills does not have to be a chore. Here are some ways to handle those monthly expenses without turning into a stress fest:

1. **Equal Contributions/Split Evenly**: Divide the total expenses right down the middle. Each partner contributes 50% of the bill amount. In this method, each partner deposits the same fixed amount into a shared account every month. This joint account is used for agreed-upon expenses, such as rent and utilities, while any remaining income is kept in individual accounts for personal spending. This setup works best for couples who earn around the same amount, as it is easy to organize and understand.

Example: If the monthly expenses are $2,000, both partners chip in $1,000 each. Easy-peasy!

2. **Proportional Contribution**: With this option, expenses are split based on the proportion of each partner's income. This approach is well-suited for couples where there is a noticeable difference in earnings, ensuring that both partners contribute fairly without putting extra strain on the lower-earning partner.

Remember that income does not just refer to salary—it could also include other sources like investments or rental income. Contribute based on your income. If one partner earns more, they pay a larger share of the bills. It is all about fairness!

Example: If Trey makes $4,000 a month and Hannah makes $2,000, they split the bills in a 2:1 ratio. Trey pays two-thirds, and Hannah pays one-third.

Example: If Dana earns $100,000 and Josh earns $60,000, Dana covers 60% of the joint expenses, while Josh covers 40%. Any remaining money stays in individual accounts.

3. **Bill Buddy System/ Expense Category Split:** In this method, each partner takes responsibility for specific categories of expenses. For example, if one partner owns the house, they might cover the mortgage and maintenance, while the other covers groceries or utilities.

Warning: This approach can often lead to confusion if not planned carefully, as it tends to develop unintentionally. Without clear agreements, it can become difficult to adjust as income and costs change over time. Assign specific bills to each partner. One takes care of the rent, and the other handles groceries and utilities.

Example: Cooper pays the rent and internet, while Diana takes care of groceries, utilities, and streaming subscriptions. They have got their system down!

4. **Hybrid - Fixed Personal Allowances:** In this approach, all income goes into a joint account, but each partner gets a fixed amount of "allowance" deposited into their personal accounts every month. The joint account is used for shared expenses, while the personal accounts allow for individual spending. This method is particularly beneficial for couples with children or one partner contributing unpaid labor, such as childcare, as it ensures equal access to personal spending money, regardless of income levels.

Example*: John and Anna*

John and Anna are married with two young kids. John works full-time as an engineer, earning $7,000 a month, while Anna stays at home and takes care of the children and household. Even though John is the primary breadwinner, they both agree that it's important for Anna to have equal access to personal spending money since her unpaid labor benefits the household. All of John's income is deposited into their joint checking account, which they use to pay for shared household expenses like the mortgage, utilities, groceries, childcare needs, and family outings. After accounting for these monthly costs, they set aside $2,000 for their personal spending. Instead of splitting the leftover funds unevenly based on income, John and Anna agree to set equal "allowances" of $1,000 each that will be deposited into their individual personal accounts.

John uses his $1,000 monthly allowance to cover his personal hobbies, dining out with friends, or buying new gadgets without needing to check in with Anna about these purchases. Despite not earning a paycheck, Anna also gets $1,000 a month for her own discretionary spending. She might use this for her yoga classes, a day at the spa, or picking up something she has been eyeing without worrying about the household budget.

Benefits to John and Anna:
Fairness: Both John and Anna have equal access to personal funds, despite the fact that John is earning the household's income. This prevents financial imbalances or resentment.

Personal Freedom: Each partner can use their personal account freely for non-essential expenses, giving them financial independence within the marriage.

Contribution Recognition: Anna's unpaid work in caring for their children and maintaining the household is recognized by ensuring she has access to spending money, even though her contributions aren't directly financial.

By using this system, John and Anna can manage household expenses responsibly while both enjoying personal spending autonomy. It is a flexible, equitable way to handle finances in relationships where one partner may not bring in an income but contributes in other significant ways.

5. **Fully Joint Account:** This method involves merging all income into a single joint account, from which all expenses are paid. There are no separate individual

accounts, although each partner can use different credit cards for personal or private purchases if agreed. This option works for couples who prefer complete financial unity, but it requires clear communication and trust to function smoothly.

Example: *Mila and Ashton*

Mila and Ashton are married, and both work full-time. Mila is a marketing manager, earning $6,000 a month, and Ashton is a software developer, bringing in $8,000 a month. They have decided to take a fully joint approach to their finances because they value transparency and financial unity in their relationship.

Mila and Ashton merge all of their income into one joint checking account. So, every month, $14,000 (the total of both their incomes) is deposited into the joint account. From this account, they pay for all of their expenses, including mortgage, utilities, groceries, dining out, Vacations, and any other shared household or personal expenses.

How It Works:
Bills and Expenses: Mila and Ashton use this joint account to cover all household expenses. Whether it's rent or groceries, everything is paid from this one account.

Personal Spending: While they do not have individual accounts, Mila and Ashton agree that they can each use their own credit cards for personal or private purchases. For example, Mila may want to buy new clothes, and Ashton might want to get a gaming console. They communicate about these expenses but don't feel the need to have separate personal accounts, as long as they respect the overall budget.

Savings: Since their incomes go into the joint account, Mila and Ashton also use it to manage their savings. They contribute to a shared emergency fund, retirement accounts, and any savings goals they may have—like buying a new car or planning a vacation.

Benefits:
Complete Unity: Mila and Ashton share every financial decision, which promotes trust and mutual understanding. By having a joint account, they stay on the same page financially.

Transparency: All income and spending are visible to both partners, which encourages open communication and prevents surprises or misunderstandings about money.

Shared Goals: This system allows Mila and Ashton to easily work toward common financial goals, like saving for a house or planning for children, without the need to balance separate accounts.

Potential Challenges:
Clear Communication: This method requires strong communication, especially for personal purchases. Both partners need to be on the same page regarding spending limits and shared goals to avoid any tension.

Trust: Since there are no personal accounts, trust plays a key role in ensuring both Mila and Ashton feel comfortable with how the money is managed and spent.

Example in Action: Mila and Ashton decide to go on a vacation, and all the costs—from flights to hotel bookings—are paid from the joint account. Mila then wants to purchase a new designer handbag, and Ashton plans to buy a set of golf clubs. They discuss these personal expenses to make sure they fit within their overall budget before using their individual credit cards. At the end of the month, they pay off the credit cards from their joint account, maintaining transparency and financial unit.

This method works for Mila and Ashton because they trust each other, communicate well about money, and feel comfortable sharing everything financially.

***

Decreasing Debt: Teamwork Makes the Dream Work

Debt can be a heavy burden but tackling it together can lighten the load. Here is how you can team up to crush that debt:

1. **Debt Snowball Method**: Focus on paying off the smallest debt first, then roll that payment into the next smallest debt. It is like building a snowball of financial freedom.

   Example: Alex and Haley start by paying off their $500 credit card debt. Once it is gone, they take that payment and apply it to their $1,500 student loan, and so on. Each victory motivates them to keep going.

2. **Debt Avalanche Method**: Pay off debts with the highest interest rates first to save money on interest. It is like an avalanche that wipes out high-interest debt.

   Example: Haley and Hal focus on their 20% interest credit card debt first. Once that's paid off, they move to the 15% interest loan. They are saving money by tackling the most expensive debt first.

3. **Shared Goals**: Set a goal to be debt-free by a certain date and celebrate each milestone together. It is like running a marathon—you pace yourselves and celebrate each checkpoint.

Example: Maria and John aim to be debt-free in five years. They set mini-goals for each debt and celebrate with a fancy dinner or a weekend getaway each time they pay one off.

***

Separation, Divorce, and Death: Navigating Life's Big Changes

Life is full of surprises, and while we hope for all good things, it is smart to prepare for the not-so-fun stuff too. Here is how a prenup can help you handle separation, divorce, and even death:

1. **Separation**: If you and your partner decide to take a break or separate, a prenup can outline how to handle your assets and responsibilities during this time. It is like having a game plan, so you do not end up in a financial tug-of-war.

In the event of a separation period, you can predetermine who will leave the marital residence, who will pay for what expenses, whether a partner will remain on the other's health insurance through the separation period, and whether any spousal support is needed for maintenance of one spouse.

2. **Divorce**: This is where a prenup really shines. It can specify how to divide property, debts, and any other financial matters. It is like having a pre-written script for an otherwise unpredictable drama, making sure things go smoothly even when emotions are high.

Now, I know divorce is not the most romantic topic, but it is essential. When emotions are high, and everything feels chaotic, that prenup is your calm, rational, pre-written script for how things should go down. It spells out exactly how to divide property, debts, and all those other financial matters that can turn a tough situation into a downright nightmare.

Example: *Kim & Kanye and A Story of a Prenup's Superpowers*

Let's imagine a famous couple, say Kim and Kanye, who are living their best life, making music, launching businesses, and building an empire together. But, as life would have it, they start to drift apart. Things get complicated, and they realize it is time to part ways. Without a prenup, their divorce could easily turn into a public spectacle—think tabloid headlines, drawn-out court battles, and enough drama to fill a season of reality TV. But wait! Kim and Kanye were smart; they had a prenup.

So, instead of a messy public feud, their prenup kicks in like a superhero, ensuring that everything is divided according to the plan they set up when they were still in love and thinking clearly. Kim knows what is hers, Kanye knows what is his, and they have even accounted for any debts. They avoid the drawn-out court process and instead, move forward with their lives, focusing on co-parenting and their individual careers.

The prenup did not just protect their wealth. It protected their peace of mind, allowing them to navigate the divorce with far less stress. In the end, the prenup turned a potentially explosive situation into a much smoother transition, proving its superpowers in real life.

3. **Death**: No one likes to think about this, but planning ahead can save a lot of stress for your loved ones. A prenup can include provisions for how assets are distributed if one of you passes away. It is about making sure your wishes are clear, and everyone knows what to expect. Think of it as a financial love letter to your future self and your loved ones, ensuring your wishes are respected and your family is taken care of.

Example: *Bella & Edward and A Twilight Tale of Planning Ahead*

Let's take a trip to Forks, Washington, where Bella and Edward are living their eternal love story. But even in a world where one partner is an immortal vampire, the realities of life—or eternal life—still require some planning.

Bella, being human, knows that her time is limited. So, they sit down and have the tough conversation. They decide to include provisions in their prenup about what should happen if one of them passes away. For Bella, it is about making sure that if something happens to her, Edward is not left dealing with financial chaos on top of his grief. For Edward, it is about ensuring that Bella, with her human fragility, is protected and that their future children (who might have a vampire-human hybrid twist) are well taken care of.

They write a financial love letter to each other through their prenup. They outline who gets what, how their assets will be divided, and how their family will be supported. Bella makes it clear that she wants certain family heirlooms to stay with her parents if something happens to her, while Edward ensures that Bella is named as the primary beneficiary for all his ancient, vampire-accumulated wealth.

By planning ahead, they have taken a huge burden off each other's shoulders. Now, they can focus on what really matters—loving each other, raising Renesmee (their half-vampire, half-human daughter), and, of course, taking down any rogue vampires that cross their path. In the end, their prenup is not just a legal document; it is a testament to their love, commitment, and the future they want to protect, no matter what.

***

The Importance of Estate Planning: Securing Your Legacy

Now, let's talk about estate planning. This is where you get to decide what happens to your stuff when you are no longer around. It is like planning your ultimate posthumous party, but with paperwork. Here is why it is important: Imagine it as planning your ultimate posthumous party—except instead of arranging for the perfect playlist and hors d'oeuvres, you are handling paperwork that ensures your stuff ends up exactly where you want it to. It might not sound glamorous, but trust me, it is crucial.

Wills and Trusts: Your Financial GPS

Wills: Think of your will as the master plan for how your assets should be distributed after you are gone. It is like drafting a map that shows exactly where you want each treasure chest (a.k.a. your belongings) to end up. Want to leave Grandma's antique vase to your cousin? Or ensure your favorite charity gets a chunk of your estate? Your will spells it all out. But remember, a will goes into effect only after you are no longer around to give directions.

Trusts: Now, trusts are like having a financial GPS for your estate. They help manage and protect your assets while you are alive and after you have moved on. It is a bit like having a butler who knows exactly where you want your assets to go and keeps them safe until the time comes to distribute them. Trusts can also help avoid the long, often costly process of probate, which is like the estate's version of waiting in a never-ending line at the DMV.

Beneficiaries: Your VIP Guest List

Who Inherits Your Assets: Your beneficiary designations are crucial because they determine who gets what when you are not around. It is like deciding which friends get the front-row seats at your concert. Make sure your beneficiary designations are current and reflect your wishes. That way, Aunt Joan does not end up with your prized baseball card collection by mistake.

Who Handles Your Affairs: You also need to name someone to handle your affairs. This is your personal party planner who will ensure everything goes smoothly when you are no longer there to call the shots. This person will step into your shoes, making sure that everything is taken care of according to your wishes.

Healthcare Directives: Your Personal Medical Playlist

Living Will: This document outlines your wishes for medical treatment if you cannot make decisions for yourself. It is like creating a playlist of your favorite tunes, so everyone knows what you want to hear. Whether you want aggressive treatment or to pass peacefully, your living will spells it out clearly.

Healthcare Power of Attorney: This appoints someone to make medical decisions on your behalf if you are unable to do so. Think of this person as your medical DJ, ensuring your preferences are respected. It is crucial to choose someone you trust completely to handle this role, as they will be making decisions in line with your wishes.

***

In essence, estate planning is all about securing your legacy with a clear, actionable plan. It ensures your wishes are followed and helps avoid any last-minute chaos. By taking these steps, you are giving your loved ones a well-organized roadmap, allowing them to focus on celebrating your life rather than scrambling to sort out your affairs. So, think of it as a gift—a final act of love and clarity that makes sure your legacy lives on just the way you intended.

Chapter 7

Creating Your Prenup

If you have made it this far, you are probably itching to roll up your sleeves and dig into the nitty-gritty of creating your prenup. Do not worry, I'm here to guide you through the process of making your prenup a reality.

Legal Guidance: The Importance of Seeking Legal Advice

Let's talk about why having a lawyer on your team is a big deal. Think of a lawyer as your prenup's personal trainer because they help make sure your agreement is in tip-top shape. But remember, not all lawyers are created equal. Make sure you share with the lawyer what YOUR goals are ... not their goals because sometimes lawyers get caught up in wanting to get a "win" for their client. You may have different definitions of winning! Make sure your overall goal is communicated clearly with your attorney and that they do not lose track of it along the way.

Here are some reasons why you should not skip this step:

1. **Expertise**: Lawyers know the ins and outs of prenups and can make sure your agreement is legally sound. They are like the GPS for your prenup journey, guiding you around any potential bumps in the road. Lawyers are seasoned navigators when it comes to prenups.

   Ins and Outs: A lawyer knows the ins and outs of prenups better than anyone. They are familiar with the legal jargon and requirements, ensuring your prenup is not only comprehensive but also legally sound. Imagine them as your GPS system, guiding you past any pitfalls and ensuring you stay on the right track. Without this expertise, you might miss crucial details or run into legal trouble down the road.

   Avoiding Problems: Just like a GPS alerts you to potential hazards on the road, a lawyer will help you sidestep common mistakes that could invalidate your prenup or create unnecessary complications. They will ensure everything is in order, so you do not have to deal with any surprises later.

2. **Customization**: A good lawyer will help tailor your prenup to fit your unique situation. It is like getting a custom-tailored suit instead of a one-size-fits-all. *This I the biggest reason everyone should seek legal counsel.* You want your prenup custom fitted to you and your relationship. An attorney can help you develop innovative strategies to achieve your desired outcome, instead of leaving you stuck with boilerplate, standard language. A one-size-fits-all approach does not work for prenups any more than it does for suits.

Tailored to You: A good lawyer will help tailor your prenup to fit your unique situation. It is like getting a custom-tailored suit instead of a generic one. This means your prenup will fit your relationship perfectly, addressing your specific concerns and goals. Whether you have a family business, special assets, or unique financial goals, a lawyer can craft an agreement that suits your needs.

Innovative Strategies: Instead of sticking with boilerplate, standard language, an attorney can help you develop innovative strategies to achieve your desired outcome. They will work with you to create a prenup that reflects your unique relationship and circumstances, rather than a cookie-cutter agreement that does not quite fit.

3. **Legal Requirements**: Different states have different laws about prenups. A lawyer will ensure your agreement meets all legal requirements, so you do not end up with a prenup that's not worth the paper it is printed on. When it comes to prenuptial agreements, the legal landscape can be as varied as the states themselves.

Just like different states have different driving laws (hello, no U-turns in NYC), each state has its own set of rules governing prenups. Understanding these nuances is crucial and how a lawyer can ensure your prenup does not end up being a glorified piece of paper.

a. State-Specific, Local Laws of Prenups

Different Stroke for Different Folks: Each state has its own legal framework for prenups, which means what is enforceable in one state might not fly in another. For example, some states may require specific language to make certain provisions valid, while others might have different rules about the disclosure of assets. It is like trying to follow traffic laws in a foreign country. What is legal in one place might be a big no-no elsewhere.

Essential Elements: States may have different requirements for a prenup to be considered valid. Common requirements include the necessity for full disclosure of assets and liabilities, the absence of coercion, and that the agreement be signed voluntarily by both parties. If these elements are not met, your prenup could be challenged in court and possibly thrown out. Imagine planning a road trip and forgetting to check the vehicle's condition, only to break down in the middle of nowhere!

b. Ensuring Validity

Navigating State-Specific Requirements: A knowledgeable lawyer is your guide through this complex maze. They will ensure that your prenup includes all the necessary elements according to your state's laws. It is like having a local tour guide who knows the best routes and shortcuts, ensuring you do not miss out on any important stops or encounter unnecessary roadblocks.

Customizing for Compliance: A lawyer will tailor your prenup to fit the legal requirements of your specific state. They will know exactly what needs to be included and how it should be worded to avoid any potential issues. This includes verifying that the document is signed and witnessed in accordance with state laws, so it is legally binding and enforceable.

Avoiding Common Pitfalls: By understanding the legal landscape, a lawyer can help you avoid common pitfalls that could invalidate your prenup. They will address potential red flags and ensure that every detail complies with state regulations. It is like having a seasoned mechanic inspect your car before a long drive, preventing problems before they arise.

Futureproofing Your Agreement by Anticipating Changes: Laws can change, and what is valid today might not be valid tomorrow. A lawyer will help you incorporate provisions that account for potential legal changes or developments in your state's laws. They will keep your prenup current and effective, just like updating your GPS with the latest maps to avoid getting lost.

Handling Disputes: If your prenup is challenged or questioned, a lawyer will be equipped to defend its validity. They will provide the necessary documentation and arguments to support the prenup's enforceability, ensuring it stands up in court. Think of them as your legal pit crew, ready to jump in and handle any issues that come up.

In essence, navigating the legal requirements for a prenup can be as tricky as figuring out the rules for a new board game. But with a lawyer by your side, you have a seasoned player who knows the ins and outs of the game. They will ensure your prenup not only meets your state's legal requirements but also stands strong against any future challenges, making sure your agreement is as solid as a rock. So, when it comes to your prenup, do not skimp on legal expertise. It is the key to making sure your agreement is worth every penny and truly protects your interests.

4. **Conflict Resolution**: If you and your partner hit any snags during the process, a lawyer can help mediate and find solutions. It is like having a referee on standby for your prenup negotiations.

***

Key Components: Essential Elements to Include in a Prenuptial Agreement

Here are the essential elements you will need to include in your prenup. The meat and potatoes, if you will:

1. **Asset Division**: Outline how you will divide your assets and debts if things do not work out. This includes property, savings, and investments. Think of it as setting the rules for a financial game.

2. **Debt Responsibilities**: Clarify who is responsible for what debt. This helps prevent any unpleasant surprises if one partner has more debt than the other. It will also define what is considered separate and marital debt, as well as how these debts will be paid during the marriage.

3. **Spousal Support**: Decide if either partner will receive spousal support (alimony) and under what conditions. It is like agreeing on the terms of a financial cushion if the relationship hits a rough patch.

4. **Estate Planning**: Include provisions for what happens to your assets if one of you passes away. It is a way of making sure your wishes are known and respected, even when you are not around. It is always a good idea to have estate planning and prenup conversations together when you can!

***

Optional and Creative Elements: Adding Your Personal Touch

Now, let's have some fun with it! Here are just some optional and creative elements you might consider adding to your prenup:

1. **Infidelity Clause**: An infidelity clause is a specific provision in a prenup that outlines the consequences if one partner is unfaithful. It is designed to offer protection and establish clear expectations regarding fidelity within the marriage. Yup, I know you have been waiting to read about the infidelity clause ... this one is a bit spicy! It is like a "cheating penalty" to keep things honest and transparent.

Example*: Blair and Nate's Story*

Blair and Nate are deeply in love and about to get married. They have decided to get a prenup to ensure clarity and protection for both of them. They trust each other but want to add an extra layer of security to their commitment. Here is how they included an infidelity clause in their prenup:

Defining Infidelity: First, they clearly define what constitutes infidelity. For Blair and Nate, infidelity is any romantic or sexual relationship outside their marriage.

Financial Penalty: If Nate cheats on Blair, he agrees to pay her $100,000. Similarly, if Blair cheats on Nate, she agrees to pay him $100,000. This amount is decided based on their mutual agreement and is meant to act as a deterrent. For example, If Nate cheats on Blair, he agrees to pay her $100,000. Similarly, if Blair cheats on Nate, she agrees to pay him $100,000. This amount is decided based on their mutual agreement and is meant to act as a deterrent.

Asset Division: The infidelity clause also affects the division of assets. If infidelity occurs, the prenup states that the innocent party receives a larger share of the marital assets. For instance, instead of a 50/50 split, the assets might be divided 70/30 in favor of the faithful partner.

Why They Chose This Clause: Blair and Nate chose an infidelity clause because it provides peace of mind and reinforces their commitment to each other, and Nate had one teeny affair with Serena when he was dating Blair. Now they have clear consequences for breaking the trust, which helps them both feel secure in their relationship.

How It Works in Practice: Let's imagine a scenario... Nate is unfaithful, and Blair discovers it. According to their prenup: Nate must pay $100,000 as a financial penalty, then the division of their marital assets will be adjusted in Blair's favor, therefore giving her 70% and Nate 30%.

Legal Validation: To activate the infidelity clause, clear evidence of infidelity would be required. This ensures fairness and prevents false accusations.

During their prenup discussion, Blair jokes, "Nate, I love you to the moon and back, but if you stray, you are paying up!"

Nate chuckles and replies, "Noted, Blair. My fidelity is worth way more than $100,000!" They both laugh, sealing their agreement with a kiss.

An infidelity clause can offer couples like Blair and Nate an additional layer of security and clarity in their marriage. By setting clear expectations and consequences, they ensure their commitment is taken seriously, all while maintaining trust and respect for each other.

2. **Insurance**: From life to auto to health insurance and everything in between ... Would you not want to know how you will handle each of these things as a couple during marriage and separation, divorce, or death? I know I certainly would!

    a. Health Insurance: For When 'In Sickness' Actually Happens.
So, you are in love and planning your future. You are ready to vow "in sickness and in health," but let's be real—

medical bills can be a mood killer. That is where a health insurance clause comes in handy! "Honey, you are worth every penny of that premium ... but let's not get sick, okay?"

Who's Covered? Your prenup can specify who is responsible for maintaining health insurance coverage. Will one of you be on the other's policy, or will you each keep your own?

Example: If Patrick's job offers stellar health insurance, the prenup might state that David will be covered under Patrick's plan. If David's job has better coverage, they might decide the other way around.

Paying the Premiums: You can decide how the premiums are split. Maybe you go 50/50, or maybe the higher earner covers a larger portion.

b. Home Insurance: Because Your Love Nest Deserves Protection.
Your home is your castle, and castles need protection. Home insurance clauses in a prenup ensure you are both clear on who has the moat and drawbridge covered.

Who is the Policyholder? Decide whose name is on the policy. Is it the homeowner, or will you both be listed?

Example: Roland owns the house, so they agree Roland will keep the home insurance in his name but add Jocelyn as an additional insured.

Splitting Costs: How will you share the cost of premiums, repairs, and deductibles?

Example: Roland and Jocelyn decide that home insurance premiums will be split 60/40, reflecting their respective incomes.

c. Auto Insurance: For When You are Cruising Through Life Together.

Cars are great until they are not. Auto insurance clauses in your prenup can help steer clear of financial wrecks.

Policy Coverage: Who is covering whom? Are you each keeping your own policy, or is one of you getting added to the other's?

Example: Homer has a sweet ride, and Marge has an old trusty sedan. They decide to keep separate policies to maintain their individual driving records.

Premium Split: How are you divvying up the costs? This can be especially important if one of you has a lead foot (you know who you are).

d. Life Insurance: Because Love Is Eternal, but Bills Are Not.

Life insurance is like a financial hug from beyond. It ensures your loved one is taken care of if the unthinkable happens.

Beneficiaries: Your prenup can specify who the beneficiary is. Usually, it is the spouse, but you can get specific.

Example: Bob and Linda agree that each will name the other as the primary beneficiary on their respective life insurance policies.

Premium Responsibilities: Decide who's paying for the policy. Maybe you both contribute to a joint policy, or you maintain separate ones.

Insurance clauses in your prenup can help you avoid financial headaches down the road. They are not exactly romantic, but they are practical. Nothing says "I love you" like making sure your partner is covered no matter what happens. So, grab a cup of coffee, sit down with your partner, and hash out these details. Future you will thank present you for being so darn responsible!

Remember, life is unpredictable, but your love is strong. With these insurance clauses, you are not just protecting your assets ... you are protecting each other.

3. **Sunset Clauses**: Think of this as a "best-by" date for your prenup. A sunset clause specifies that the prenup will expire after a certain number of years, allowing you to review and update it if needed. It is like setting a reminder to reassess your agreement down the road.

Serving like an expiration date for your prenup, a sunset clause is like saying, "This part of the agreement is only valid until a certain point in time, after which it goes away. Poof!" This can help couples feel more comfortable with the prenup, because certain terms do not last forever, just until a certain milestone in their marriage.

Example: *Susan and Denise's Story*

Susan and Denise are about to tie the knot, and they have decided to get a prenup. They are both super excited but also want to make sure they are being smart about their future. Susan has a flourishing online business, and Denise has some significant savings from her years as an architect. They want to protect their individual assets but also show their commitment to a long-lasting marriage, so they set up a sunset clause.

Initial Terms: The prenup states that if Susan and Denise divorce within the first five years of marriage, they each keep the assets they brought into the marriage. Susan's business remains hers, and Denise's savings stay with her

The Sunset Clause: The prenup includes a sunset clause that says, "If Susan and Denise remain married for five years, the provisions regarding the separate ownership of premarital assets will expire."

After Five Years: If Susan and Denise are still happily married on their fifth anniversary, the clause about keeping their premarital assets separate dissolves. From this point on, any division of assets will be based on what they have acquired together, without special consideration for their premarital assets.

Why Did Susan and Denise Choose This Sunset Clause? Susan and Denise chose a sunset clause because it felt fair and gave them both a sense of security. They are committed to their marriage and feel that after five years, they will be a strong enough team to not need the extra protection.

How Does it Work in Practice? Let's look at their fifth anniversary:

Before Anniversary: If they had divorced before the five-year mark, Susan's business would remain hers, and Denise's savings would stay with her.

After Anniversary: Since they are celebrating five wonderful years together, the sunset clause kicks in. Now, their prenup no longer has provisions about their premarital assets. Any financial decisions moving forward are based on what they have built together during their marriage.

On their fifth anniversary, Susan jokes, "Well, looks like my business is officially *our* business now!"

Denise laughs and adds, "And my savings are now our savings! Cheers to us!" They clink their glasses, knowing they have built a solid foundation for their future.

A sunset clause can be a fantastic way for couples to ease into a prenup, knowing that certain terms will not last forever. For Susan and Denise, it provided initial security and later transitioned them into a unified financial future. It is all about finding what works best for both partners and making sure everyone feels comfortable and protected.

4. **Lifestyle Clauses**: Here is where you can get a bit creative. For example, a clause might state that if one partner gains a certain amount of weight, the couple will agree to a specific action, like attending a fitness class together. (Note: This is more about fun and motivation than serious enforcement.)

Example: *A Big Weight Gain Alimony Clause*

Have you heard the true story about a ten-pound clause in a prenup? Here is a simplified version. Once upon a time, in the land of prenups and legal lingo, there was a wealthy businessman, let's call him Mr. Big. Mr. Big was engaged to a lovely woman named Carrie. They were madly in love and excited about their future together. However, Mr. Big, being a meticulous and somewhat controlling individual, insisted on having a prenuptial agreement before they tied the knot.

Mr. Big's prenup was not your ordinary document. Among the usual clauses about asset division and spousal support, there was one clause that stood out like a sore thumb. This clause stipulated that if Carrie gained more than 10 pounds during their marriage, Mr. Big's alimony payments to her would decrease proportionally with each pound gained.

Carrie did not remember watching her friend Charlotte's past prenup negotiations. In her love-struck state and trusting Mr. Big's intentions, Carrie agreed to the prenup without fully considering the implications of this peculiar clause. They got married in a grand ceremony, and for a while, life was blissful.

As time went by, the realities of married life set in. Carrie found herself juggling multiple responsibilities and dealing with stress. Naturally, her weight did fluctuate a bit. Mr. Big, ever the stickler for details, began to take note. He became increasingly fixated on Carrie's weight, reminding her of the prenup clause whenever he felt she was gaining a little.

This constant pressure took a toll on Carrie. The stress of trying to maintain her weight, combined with Mr. Big's obsessive behavior, strained their relationship. She felt like she was being controlled and judged, rather than loved and supported.

Eventually, the tension became too much, and the couple decided to divorce. During the proceedings, the infamous weight clause came into play. Carrie's attorney argued that the clause was unreasonable, invasive, and unenforceable. They contended that such a clause violated Carrie's personal rights and dignity.

The judge presiding over the case disagreed. The weight clause was upheld as valid! Though Mr. Big was criticized for being a jerk, in the end, the entire prenup was upheld. The court found the weight-clause disgusting, but it was part of a valid contract that they both agreed to and signed.

The Moral of the Story: The story of Mr. Big and Carrie is a perfect example of what not to do when creating a prenuptial agreement. Clauses that control personal aspects of a partner's life, like weight, can lead to significant emotional distress and legal challenges. Prenups should focus on fair and equitable terms that respect both parties' autonomy and dignity.

5. **Pet Custody**: If you and your partner share a love for furry, feathered, or scaly friends, you might want to consider including a pet custody clause in your prenup. Think of it as a custody agreement for your beloved pets, ensuring they get the love and care they deserve, no matter what happens down the road.

Pets are more than just animals. They are family members with personalities, quirks, and a whole lot of love. So, when it comes to a potential split, having a clear plan for your pets can help avoid disputes and ensure they are cared for according to their needs and your wishes. After all, who wants to argue over their beloved pup's future when they are already dealing with a breakup?

Example*: Mutt and Twyla Get a Dog*

Mutt, a charmingly disheveled guy with a heart of gold, and Tywla, a quirky, lovable woman who runs the local café have been together for a few years and have a beloved, albeit mischievous, Golden Retriever named Rufus. Mutt and Tywla are both deeply attached to Rufus. He is their constant companion on hikes, a snuggler on the couch, and even the unofficial greeter at the cafe. But as their relationship hits a rough patch, they realize it is time to have "the talk"—and this time, it is not about their feelings, but about Rufus's future.

Mutt and Tywla decide to add a pet custody clause to their prenup. They want to ensure that Rufus is cared for and has a stable home, regardless of what happens between them.

First, they create a custody clause. They agree that if they ever separate, Tywla will have primary custody of Rufus, given that he spends most of his time at the cafe, which is more familiar to him. This arrangement considers Rufus's current environment and routine, ensuring a smooth transition.

Along with this custody, Mutt and Twyla agree on visitation rights. Mutt will have the right to visit Rufus on weekends and holidays. They both want Mutt to stay involved in Rufus's life, so they outline specific times for visitation and activities they can do together. Think of it like setting up Rufus's weekend plans—parks, treats, and all.

Even though Rufus spends most time with Twyla, the two also agree that Mutt will contribute to Rufus's vet bills and food costs, ensuring that he continues to receive high-quality care. It is like setting up a shared bank account for Rufus's needs, so neither party is burdened with unexpected expenses alone.

If something happens to both of them, they designate a trusted friend, David, to step in as Rufus's guardian. They want to ensure Rufus has a loving home even if they are not around, making sure Rufus's future is secured no matter what.

By including these details in their prenup, Mutt and Tywla not only clarify their expectations but also avoid potential disputes. It ensures that Rufus's well-being is prioritized and that both Mutt and Tywla have peace of mind knowing their furry friend will be cared for and will not be lost in the shuffle of a breakup.

Including a pet custody clause in your prenup is a thoughtful way to address the needs of your beloved pets. It is not just about who gets the couch and who gets the bed, but is about ensuring that your furry friends are taken care of with the same love and attention you have given them. Just like Mutt and Tywla, having a clear plan can make a tough situation a bit easier and ensure that your pets are always in good hands. After all, they are not just pets—they are family, and they deserve to be part of your thoughtful planning.

***

What A lawyer Can Help You With

I need to remind you about getting a lawyer to draft or review your prenup again, because it is just that important. A lawyer is going to be your guiding star through this process. Here is how they will help:

1. **Drafting the Agreement**: They will put all the agreed-upon terms into a legally binding document. It is like turning your prenup ideas into a formal contract, rather than a stack of bar napkins from when you had a financial talk.

2. **Ensuring Fairness**: A lawyer will make sure that the terms are fair to both parties and comply with state laws. They are like the fairness referee, ensuring everything is balanced.

3. **Navigating Negotiations**: They will assist with negotiating terms and resolving any disagreements. It is like having a skilled negotiator on your team to help find common ground.

4. **Final Review**: Before you sign, a lawyer will review the final draft to ensure everything is in order. It is like getting a final check-up before heading to the wedding altar.

***

Begin the Conversation: How to Bring Up the Idea of a Prenup

Starting the conversation about a prenup can feel like opening a can of worms, but it does not have to be scary. I have some tips in earlier chapters on how to start the conversation. Here are some more ideas on how to bring it up with ease:

1. **Choose the Right Moment**: Pick a calm, relaxed time to discuss the prenup. Avoid bringing it up during a stressful moment, like right before a big family dinner. It is like choosing the right time to talk about vacation plans—make sure it is a good moment for both of you.

2. **Be Honest and Open**: Explain why you think a prenup is a good idea and how it can benefit both of you. Approach it as a practical discussion, not a personal attack. Think of it as a planning session for your future, not a critique of your relationship.

3. **Use "We" Language**: Frame it as something you both can benefit from and work on together. For example, "Maybe a prenup could help us avoid potential conflicts and ensure *we* are *both* protected. What do you think?"

4. **Keep it Light**: Try to keep the conversation light and positive. Maybe you use a bit of humor, or maybe you choose a light moment to bring it up.

***

Negotiations: What Are They, Why Are They Important, and Beginning the Process

Negotiations are where you and your partner hash out the details of the prenup. Maybe you already have a prenup drafted, or you are about to.

1. **What Are They?** Negotiations involve discussing and agreeing on the terms of the prenup. It is like having a friendly debate to figure out the best way to handle things.

2. **Why Are They Important?** Negotiations ensure that both parties have a say in the prenup and that the terms are fair and mutually agreed upon. It is about making sure everyone's voice is heard and that the agreement reflects both partners' wishes.

3. **Starting the Process**: Begin by discussing your priorities and concerns. Use the Prenup Goals Worksheet from the appendix to guide your conversation. Be open, honest, and willing to compromise. It is like working on a project together. Collaborate to create something that works for both of you.

Imagine you and your partner are in a serious prenup negotiation, and one of you says, "How about we add a clause about who gets the last slice of pizza?" It is a funny reminder that while the prenup is important, keeping things lighthearted can help make the process smoother.

Creating your prenup might seem like a daunting task, but with the right guidance and a little humor, it can be a positive experience. Seek legal advice, include the essential and optional elements that matter to you, and have open, honest conversations with your partner. Remember, a prenup is about protecting both of you and setting the stage for a happy future together.

Grab that Prenup Goals Worksheet, have those conversations, and let's make sure your prenup is as smooth as your love story. You've got this!

Conclusion

The Prenup Girl's final word on prenups, because happily ever after deserves a safety net:

You have made it to the end and let me just say: *bravo!* You have tackled the tough conversations, dodged financial landmines, and maybe even had a couple of "Wait, what?!" moments along the way. But hey, that is all part of the journey—just like when Ross and Rachel had to "go on a break" before realizing they belonged together. So now that you are armed with all this prenup preparation power, let's go over the highlights, shall we?

1. Communication is Your Relationship-Saver.

Whether you are a Monica and Chandler or a Jim and Pam, one thing is clear: communication is the secret sauce to any lasting relationship. Your prenup is just the start of those deep convos. You have learned how to talk about the hard stuff—money, debt, goals—and now you can walk into marriage knowing you are both on the same page (or at least the same book).

Like Carrie Bradshaw once said, *"Some people are settling down, some people are settling, and some people refuse to settle for anything less than butterflies."* You are not settling at all. In fact, you are planning smart and protecting your heart ... and assets.

2. A Prenup is Your Ultimate Peace of Mind.

Think of a prenup as your relationship insurance policy. We all hope for the best, but sometimes, life throws in a plot twist that even Shonda Rhimes would not dare to write. And guess what? You will be ready. Whether it is planning for "what if" or "just in case," you have got the safety net in place.

3. Love + Logic = A Power Couple Move

Remember, a prenup does not mean you are expecting a divorce, Rather, it means you are planning for a strong, secure future. It is like Monica having backup lasagna in the freezer—no one *expects* to need it, but when things get heated, you will be grateful it is there.

If Beyoncé taught us anything, it is to be independent while still being in love. Queen B said, "If you liked it then you shoulda put a ring on it," and if you are smart, you will add a prenup too.

4. Your Prenup, Your Story.

The beauty of a prenup is that it is all about *your* relationship, your goals, and your unique love story. You are writing your own script, so make sure it has the perfect balance of romance and realism. Don't settle for a one-size-fits-all agreement, tailor it like the fabulous, custom suit it is.

5. Money Doesn't Have to Be a Dealbreaker.

We have all seen it in the movies—the couple breaks up over money issues, one big blowout argument after another (*cue the dramatic music*). But guess what? That does not have to be you. You have handled the hard talks, planned your future, and now you can focus on what really matters: living your best life together.

***

And So, My Lovebirds...

You did it. You are ready to walk down the aisle with more than just *the dress* on your mind. You have got your future, your finances, and your fabulous self covered. Whether you are planning to live in a chic downtown loft like Jess and Nick or build a mini-empire like Chuck and Blair, you are doing it with confidence, communication, and a rock-solid prenup.

So here is to love, here is to laughter, and here is to a lifetime of having each other's backs—no matter what. Now go slay that wedding day, and do not forget: A prenup is not just smart, it is chic.

**XOXO,
The Prenup Girl**

Appendix A:
Prenup Goals Worksheet

[Check all that apply; highlight or mark those that are most important to you]

Property Ownership

[ ] 1. Keep my **premarital** assets separate.
    Exceptions:

[ ] 2. Have the following assets **acquired during marriage** considered separate property, marital property, or community property:

    <u>Separate</u>   <u>Marital</u>   <u>Community</u>

a. Real estate purchased
    [ ]   [ ]   [ ]

b. Each person's salary earned during marriage
    [ ]   [ ]   [ ]

c. My retirement benefits earned during our marriage
    [ ]   [ ]   [ ]

d. Stock options and other employment benefits
    [ ]   [ ]   [ ]

e. Any increase in the value of a premarital business
    [ ]   [ ]   [ ]

f. Other investments
    [ ]   [ ]   [ ]

g. Joint bank accounts
    [ ]   [ ]   [ ]

h. Other: _____
    [ ]   [ ]   [ ]
    Comments: _____

i. Other: _____
    [ ]   [ ]   [ ]
    Comments: _____

j. Other: _____
    [ ]   [ ]   [ ]
    Comments: _____

[ ] 3. Include the following special provisions regarding assets acquired during marriage: _____

Debts
[ ] 4. Protect one or both of us from the other person's premarital debts.

[ ] 5. Protect one or both of us from the other person's business debts or other debts incurred during marriage.

Financial Responsibilities During Marriage
[ ] 6. Specify a process for filing income tax returns each year.

[ ] 7. Specify each person's responsibility for household expenses.

[ ] 8. Other: _____

Estate Planning
[ ] 9. Provide for one or both of our children from another relationship.

[ ] 10. Provide for our children.

[ ] 11. Pass on family property.

[ ] 12. Avoid disagreements between my spouse and my other heirs after my death by including certain terms in my estate plan.

[ ] 13. Provide for my support if my spouse dies.

[ ] 14. Provide for my spouse when I die.

Divorce
[ ] 15. Avoid an expensive and complicated divorce by deciding property issues in advance.

[ ] 16. Specify that I [*choose one:* will/will not] receive alimony if we get divorced

Other Goals

[ ] 17. Sunset Clause - After a passage of time, you can make your entire prenup or specific clauses of our prenup expire.

[ ] 18. Infidelity Clause.

[ ] 19. Pet rights.

[ ] 20. Attorney's fees.

[ ] 21. Social Image.

[ ] 22. _____

Appendix B:
Couple's Prenup Quiz

Grab your partner and some coffee, tea, wine, or something stronger. Go through this quiz together and figure out what financial future you want to have in your marriage. Once you discuss and fill this out, your attorney's will thank you! If you enter into conversations with a lawyer to write your prenup, already being on the same page with your partner is going to help you save time and money.

1. PREMARITAL ASSETS: As a couple, we want our premarital assets (*any assets acquired and earned PRIOR to the marriage*) to be one of the following:

[ ] SEPARATE PROPERTY - *AKA: what you bring into the marriage stays your separate property during the marriage... just don't commingle your separate property with marital property after marriage. Summary: "What's mine stays mine, and what's yours stays yours, plus any extras that come from those things." – See Chapter 3, Approach #1 to learn more!*

[ ] MARITAL PROPERTY - *AKA: what you both bring into the marriage becomes part of the shared marital estate. Summary: "This is the ultimate "what's mine is yours" strategy." – See Chapter 3, Approach #2 to learn more!*

[ ] HYBRID APPROACH - *Exceptions or special provisions - This is when you want some premarital assets to remain separate and some to be shared in the marriage; AKA: We want a mixture. Summary: ""What's mine is mine, but any growth or new goodies we get from it, we share." – See Chapter 3, Approach #3 to learn more!*

Describe in detail below any other thoughts on how to manage your premarital assets.

2. **ASSETS ACQUIRED DURING THE MARRIAGE.** *Unless your prenup says otherwise, as a general rule in some states, assets acquired during the marriage are considered marital or community property by default. Use this section to designate if you'd like to depart from the traditional classification and want to specifically designate one of the following assets as separate property, martial, or community property.* Choose how to specifically designate the following assets acquired <u>during</u> your marriage:

	Separate	Marital	Community
a.	Real estate purchased (with marital funds)		
	[ ]	[ ]	[ ]
b.	Client's salary/income earned during marriage		
	[ ]	[ ]	[ ]
c.	Partner's salary/income earned during marriage		
	[ ]	[ ]	[ ]
d.	Retirement benefits earned during our marriage		
	[ ]	[ ]	[ ]
e.	Stock options and other employment benefits earned during our marriage		
	[ ]	[ ]	[ ]
f.	Any increase in the value of a premarital business		
	[ ]	[ ]	[ ]
g.	Other investments		
	[ ]	[ ]	[ ]
h.	Joint bank accounts		
	[ ]	[ ]	[ ]
i.	Other: _____		
	[ ]	[ ]	[ ]

j.   Other: _____
     [ ]   [ ]   [ ]
k.   Other: _____
     [ ]   [ ]   [ ]
l.   Other: _____
     [ ]   [ ]   [ ]

3. Additional special provisions concerning assets acquired during marriage.
   Details:

4. Discuss any current debts over $500. Write the three most significant debts below (Account, Approximate Amount Owed), and if you want to separately or jointly assume/pay these debts.
   Partner 1:

   Partner 2:

5. If either of you have a premarital business, please list the business and include how you would like to classify the business upon marriage (separate, martial, or a hybrid approach). Consider how you both may want to *value* the business in the event of divorce. Consider how you may want to *split* a business in the event of divorce.
   Partner 1:

Partner 2:

6. If either of you contemplate ever starting a business during the marriage, discuss how you would like to classify the business during marriage (separate, martial, or a hybrid approach). Consider how you both may want to *value* the business in the event of divorce. Consider how you may want to split a business in the event of divorce.
    Partner 1:

    Partner 2:

7. Your prenup will spell out a process for deciding whether to file joint tax returns and how to allocate income, deductions, taxes, and refunds. Notate how you will file taxes and handle the other tax related issues.
    Details:

8. Your prenup can define each person's responsibility for household expenses. Use the first section if you will have a joint payment plan, otherwise, designate who will make what payments. If you are paying separately for different expenses, note that below and how you'd prefer to handle expenses in the

marriage. OR if you disagree with how to split expenses, notate how you would you each prefer to split expenses, and your attorneys can weigh in or try to find a middle ground option for you. *See Chapter 6, Paying the Bills and Sharing the Load for some examples on how you can split expenses.*

Details for joint payment:

Partner 1:

Partner 2:

8.   Your prenup can support an intended estate plan (this might require waivers of surviving spouse rights). Do you plan to do estate planning? If so, what are some of the specifics you'd like it to address? Details:

Partner 1:

Partner 2:

9. Your prenup will specify what should happen to your property if you separate and divorce, if not already mentioned. Please include any specific provisions you'd like included.

Partner 1:

Partner 2:

10. Your prenup can limit, avoid, or provide for alimony if we separate and divorce. *In the event of divorce, if one spouse is the "supporting spouse" in the marriage, it's possible there will be a requirement to pay for the needs of the "dependent spouse." A dependent spouse may be a stay-at-home partner or just a spouse with a significantly lower earning capacity.* Discuss scenarios that may make one spouse supporting or dependent and how you'd like to handle it in the event of divorce.

Partner 1:

Partner 2:

11. Your prenup can include other agreements that apply if you divorce. *For instance, you could include who would move from the marital home, how gets specific martial assets, etc.*

12. Other provisions of your prenup. Write down any ideas you both have that you want to ask about or discuss with a lawyer. You don't know if you don't ask!

Appendix C

Stay Connected with The Prenup Girl!

The journey does not stop here. If you're loving the tips, stories, and advice from The Prenup Girl, make sure to follow me for even more fun, updates, and behind-the-scenes moments! Whether you're knee-deep in wedding planning, navigating the early days of marriage, or just here for some real talk about love and life, let's stay connected.

Follow me on **Instagram @PrenupGirl** for more inspo, wedding planning tips, and all things love (and prenups, of course)! And you can follow the main law firm page @StriveLawFirm

Get the latest tips and mini-lessons with a side of fun over on **TikTok @ThePrenupGirl**

Visit the **blog at https://strivelawfirm.com/the-blog** for weekly posts about everything from prenups to wedding venues!

the prenup girl
WITH STRIVE LAW FIRM

The Prenup Girl's Top Wedding Planning App Recommendation:

Alright, lovebirds, you've got the ring, the date, and by now, the prenup (hopefully). But what about everything else? That's where Zola comes in to save the day. If you haven't heard of Zola, let me introduce you to your new wedding planning BFF. Zola is *the* all-in-one wedding planning app and website that makes organizing your big day a total breeze.

From setting up your wedding website to creating the most stress-free gift registry known to mankind, Zola has you covered. Need a venue? A photographer? Invitations? Boom—Zola's got a database full of vendors just waiting for you. It's basically like having a personal wedding assistant, minus the constant texting.

Trust me, whether you're a Type A planner or more of a "figure it out as we go" kind of bride, Zola is the secret weapon you didn't know you needed. So if you're looking to plan your dream wedding without losing your mind, head over to Zola's website and get started. Thank me later!

Printed in the USA
CPSIA information can be obtained
at www.ICGtesting.com
LVHW090858221124
797033LV00009BB/724